Munich

D0828095

Berlitz Publishing Company, Inc.
Princeton Mexico City London Eschborn Singapore

Copyright © 2001 Berlitz Publishing Company, Inc.
400 Alexander Park, Princeton, NJ, 08540 USA
9-13 Grosvenor St., London, W1K 4QA UK

All rights reserved. No part of this book may be reproduced or transmitted in any form or by any means, electronic or mechanical, including photocopying, recording or by any information storage or retrieval system without permission in writing from the publisher.

Berlitz Trademark Reg. U.S. Patent Office and other countries
Marca Registrada

Original Text: Jack Altman
Revised by: Karen Coe
Photography: Chris Coe
Cover Photo: Chris Coe
Layout: Media Content Marketing, Inc.
Cartography: Raffaele De Gennaro

Although the publisher tries to insure the accuracy of all the information in this book, changes are inevitable and errors may result. The publisher cannot be responsible for any resulting loss, inconvenience, or injury. If you find an error in this guide, please let the editors know by writing to Berlitz Publishing Company, 400 Alexander Park, Princeton, NJ 08540-6306.

ISBN 2-8315-7821-3

Printed in Italy
010/107 REV

CONTENTS

• A ☛ in the text denotes a highly recommended sight

Munich

S
U

THE CITY AND ITS PEOPLE

With its relaxed lifestyle, Munich seems almost Mediterranean. For many European travelers, this last main stop before the Alps provides a first breath of Italy.

Munich, the Bavarian capital, is more Baroque than Gothic and more green than gray.

Munich's genius has always been its ability to combine the Germanic talent for getting things done with a specifically Bavarian need to do them pleasantly. Business lunches seem to last a little longer here, and office hours seem to be a little shorter. Yet no one who has witnessed the city's impressive affluence, its dynamic car industry, and its splendid underground system would suggest that this delightfully relaxed attitude was unproductive.

If the people of Munich do differ so much from other Germans, that is because, you'll be told, this isn't Germany, it's Bavaria. As the capital of the fervently Catholic and conservative Free State of Bavaria, Munich epitomizes the independent Bavarian spirit. Here, good-natured local chauvinism knows no bounds—jokes about stiff-necked Prussians are common. At the city's renowned Oktoberfest, the annual beer festival, visitors sing "Warum ist es am Rhein so schön?" ("Why is it so lovely on the Rhine?") to the great amusement of the locals who, they say, don't have to ask themselves why Bavaria is so lovely.

The Oktoberfest is, perhaps, what first strikes the popular imagination in relation to Munich. Indeed, with annual consumption of 5,000,000 litres of beer by 6,000,000 visitors, it is a grandiose event, quite appropriate to the oversized image the Bavarians have of their capital. It is also the most extravagant expression of that untranslatable feeling of warm

Fisherman Fountain in Marienplatz, a good place to read... or talk on the phone.

fellowship known in German as *Gemütlichkeit*.

But it would be wrong to think of life in Munich merely as one long Oktoberfest. As a result of the post war division of Berlin, Munich became the undisputed cultural capital of the Federal Republic of Germany—no mean achievement, in the face of the considerable claims of Hamburg, Frankfurt, and Cologne. The opera house and concert halls make the town a musical mecca still, especially for the performance of works by Mozart, Wagner, and Richard Strauss.

Painters also appreciate the favorable artistic climate of the city, particularly in the bohemian district of Schwabing, which exploded onto the international scene in the 20th century as a center for the Blaue Reiter school, whose ranks included Wassily Kandinsky, Paul Klee, and Franz Marc. Munich still has some of the world's most innovative galleries, as well as the superbly displayed classical and modern collections of the Alte and Neue Pinakothek museums, both of which are richly endowed. The Pinakothek der Moderne, another stunning museum, is scheduled to open in the year 2002.

Munich has become a center for industry and publishing, and also for the much-admired New German Cinema and its world-famous directors, Volker Schloendorff, Werner Herzog, and Edgar Reitz.

But there is also a darker side to the city, including Adolf Hitler's early association with Munich and the formation here of the Nazi Party. The stormy years from 1918 to 1945 were, in the end, a brief political interlude for Munich, and its people seem happy to have relinquished the political spotlight to Bonn and Berlin.

Munich has tried, however, to retain its historical identity. After the destruction resulting from World War II, many German cities decided to break with the past and rebuild in a completely modern style. But the Bavarian capital preferred to painstakingly restore and reconstruct the

Prost! Revelers raise their glasses to Bavarian musicians at Hofbräuhaus.

great churches and palaces of its past. There are plenty of modern skyscrapers, but the heart of the old city has authentically recaptured its Baroque charm. Some people thought that the reconstruction and renovation were too thorough, too "clean," but now, a few decades later, the ravages of pollution have given the new-old buildings a patina of age that it used to take centuries to acquire. In fact, because the city's reconstruction has been so complete and so convincing, monuments such as the Siegestor (Victory Gate) have been left in their bomb-scarred condition as a history lesson.

The inner city is a pedestrian's delight, thanks both to a clever road system that keeps the majority of the traffic circling the city center rather than crossing through it (except by means of underpasses) and to an excellent system of public transport. Beyond the city center the broad, tree-lined avenues and boulevards planned by Bavaria's last kings open up the town and provide a considerable touch of elegance.

The Englischer Garten, immensely enhanced by the ebullient River Isar, is a veritable jewel among Europe's great parks. The river's swiftly flowing waters are evidence of the proximity of the Alps, where the river has its source. On a clear day, the mountains seem to lie just beyond the city's southern suburbs. That's when the *Föhn* is blowing; this famous wind gives some a headache and inspires others with phenomenally clear creative insights—a characteristic Munich ambiguity.

When the mountains appear on the city's doorstep, they remind the people of the countryside from which many of them, or their parents, came. Every weekend there is a massive exodus to the surrounding villages and lakes: east to the Chiemsee; west and south to the Ammersee, Starnberger See, and Tegernsee; and northward to Schleissheim and

Freising. Here the citizens of Munich can indulge in hiking, sailing, hunting, and fishing, or visiting aunts and uncles for coffee and cakes.

In the winter, they trek farther south into the mountains for skiing, an integral part of Munich life. Although Munich is undoubtedly a metropolis, and in many ways a sophisticated one, the city also retains a resolutely rural atmosphere, never losing sight of its origins in the hinterland. Visitors can easily participate in Munich's happy mixture of town and country.

Animated conversation is a common occurence in Munich, often taking place over mugs of local beer.

A BRIEF HISTORY

Munich was a late arrival on the Bavarian scene. During the Middle Ages, at a time when Nuremberg, Augsburg, and Regensburg were already thriving cities, the present-day state capital was just a small settlement housing a few peasants and some Benedictine monks from Lake Tegern. The site was known in the eighth century quite simply as *Ze den Munichen,* a dialect form of *zu den Mönchen* (the monks' place). Accordingly, Munich's coat of arms today bears the image of a child in a monk's habit, the Münchner Kindl.

In 1156, the settlement of the River Isar attracted the attention of Heinrich der Löwe (Henry the Lion), the Duke of Saxony and Bavaria, who was cousin of the German Emperor Frederick Barbarossa. He was looking for a place to set up a toll station for the passage of salt, a lucrative product from nearby Salzburg. Until then, tolls had been collected by the powerful bishop of Freising at Oberföhring Bridge, just to the north. Duke Heinrich burned this bridge down, and built a new one, together with a market, customs house, and mint, at a fork in the Isar.

Bishop Otto of Freising was himself an uncle of Frederick Barbarossa, and protested to the emperor, who decided to leave Munich in Heinrich's hands, but to grant one-third of the toll revenues to the diocese of Freising—dues that were paid until 1852. The day of the emperor's decision, 14 June 1158, is recognized as the date of Munich's founding.

The salt trade made Munich prosperous, and the settlement grew rapidly into a town. In 1180, after Heinrich refused military aid for the emperor's foreign wars, Frederick Barbarossa threatened to raze Munich to the ground. However, Bishop Otto pleaded the city's case, as he was making a great deal of money from his share of the salt duty. Munich was saved, but the city was handed over to the Wittelsbach family, who ruled Bavaria for the next seven centuries.

The Wittelsbachs Take Over

By the end of the 13th century, Munich was the largest town in the Wittelsbach dominions. However, the prosperous Munich burghers grew discontented and began to press Duke Ludwig the Stern (1229–1294) for a larger piece of the pie. In defense, the duke built himself a fortress, the Alter Hof, parts of which can still be seen just west of the Hofbräuhaus.

Munich entered the international political arena in 1328, when Duke Ludwig IV (1294–1347) was made Holy Roman Emperor. With his court firmly established in Munich, he enlisted scholars from all over Europe as his advisors. Perhaps the most notable of these were Marsiglio of Padua and William of Occam, philosophers who defended secular power against that of the Pope and thus made themselves useful allies for Ludwig. William of Occam became famous for "Occam's Razor," in which he states, roughly, that if you've found a simple explanation for a problem, don't look for a complicated one. The Bavarians like that kind of thinking.

Troubled Times

The Black Death brought devastation to Munich in 1348. The city suffered social unrest, abrupt economic decline, and the debasement of its currency. In an irrational reaction to the catastrophe, citizens went on a wild rampage, massacring Jews for alleged ritual murder.

High taxes and widespread penury caused the burghers to revolt against the patricians. In 1385, the people took a cloth merchant, Hans Impler, from his house to the Schrannenplatz (now Marienplatz) and beheaded him. The patricians and their princes demanded financial compensation, and the situation deteriorated into open rebellion from 1397 to 1403.

By bringing in heavy military reinforcements, the Wittelsbachs regained the upper hand without being forced to make any of the far-reaching civic concessions won by the guilds of other German towns such as Augsburg, Hamburg, and Cologne. To secure their position during these troubled times, the Wittelsbachs built a sturdy Residenz on what was then the northwest corner of town. The massive, fortress-like palace (see page 42) attests to the level of protection needed to keep this despotic monarchy safe from its own people.

Reform and Counter-Reform

Dissent eased in the 15th century, and trade boomed in salt, wine, and cloth. The town also served as a transit point for the rich "Venice goods" of spices and gold. The great Frauenkirche, still a town symbol, as well as the Gothic civic citadel of the Altes Rathaus, were built during this period of renewed prosperity.

By the middle of the 16th century, an architectural rivalry had grown up between the burghers, who favored the German Gothic style for their homes, and the Bavarian nobles, who preferred the Renaissance styles of Spain and Italy. The appearance of Munich in the 1500s is preserved in Jakob Sandtner's city model on display in the Bavarian National Museum (see page 54). However, most of the original buildings were later replaced by the Baroque and Rococo palaces of the 17th and 18th centuries and the Neo-Gothic and Neo-Classical buildings of the Industrial Revolution.

The Bavarian aristocracy's preference for foreign styles was in many ways a reaction to the subversive implications of German nationalism, which had grown out of the Reformation. In 1510, when Martin Luther passed through Munich on his way to Rome, his still relatively orthodox preaching met with sympathy. But some ten years later Luther's revolutionary position aroused the anger of the traditionally conservative Bavarians, and Duke Wilhelm IV introduced the severe measures advocated by the Jesuits. Rebellious monks and priests were arrested and executed. In 1527, the repression culminated in the drowning or burning of 29 members of Munich's Baptist community who refused to recant.

The religious conflict concealed a competition for political and economic power. The city's bourgeoisie had seen in the Reformation an opportunity to push for the social reforms which the aristocracy had adamantly resisted. In the struggles that followed, the burghers were forced to relinquish the salt monopoly to the administration of the state.

With a certain vindictiveness, the nobles flaunted their political triumph with sumptuous festivities at court, such as those arranged to pay homage to Emperor Charles V and his Spanish retinue during their Munich visit of 1530. The climax of such pomp and circumstance in grand Renaissance style was the three-week-long wedding celebration of Duke Wilhelm V and his bride, Renata of Lorraine, in 1568.

Altes Rathaus, the city's Gothic civic citadel, was built in the 15th century.

The patricians received spiritual support from the Jesuits, who were brought to Munich by Duke Wilhelm V to establish a school and to set up a theater for the performance of morality plays. Some people resented this influence, laying the foundation for the now perennial Bavarian distrust of outsiders.

Good Money After Bad

Such extravagant expenditure meant that the state coffers were empty by the time Maximilian I (1573–1651) came to the throne. Even though the Bavarian state was now almost completely bankrupt, Maximilian (who was made Prince Elector in 1623) proceeded to build up a magnificent collection of art works. However painful this may have been for his tax-crippled subjects, we can be thankful to him for having thus laid the foundations of the Alte Pinakothek.

Inside the Residenz, the fortress-like palace built by the Wittelsbachs to protect themselves from the citizens.

It was also Maximilian who ordered the splendid decorations that embellish the Residenz. Gustavus Adolphus of Sweden, who invaded Munich in 1632 during the cruel Thirty Years' War, was so impressed with the Residenz that he said he would have liked to carry the whole thing back to Stockholm on wheels. Instead, he settled for 42 Munich citizens, who were taken hostage against payment by Bavaria of 300,000 Thaler in war reparations. (All but six of them returned three years later.)

In the Thirty Years' War (1618–1648), bombardment damage was less in Munich than in many other German towns. However, starvation and disease wrought more havoc than the cannon. In 1634 the Black Death struck, taking a toll of 7,000 inhabitants, one-third of the city's population. In 1638, Maximilian set up the Mariensäule (Column of the Virgin Mary) as thanks for the town's deliverance from suffering.

Munich's Prince Electors frequently involved the city in costly foreign adventures, thus rubbing salt into the wounds of civic poverty. In 1683, Max II Emmanuel decided to help the Austrians beat off the Turks besieging Vienna. He promptly set out for Belgrade, and returned bringing 296 Turks as sedan-chair bearers and road-builders—Munich's first *Gastarbeiter* (immigrant workers). The Turkish Wars are commemorated in huge paintings that are on display in Schleissheim Castle. The city was saddled with an immense debt as a result of the war.

During the War of the Spanish Succession (1701–1714) Max Emmanuel fought on the losing side, with the French, and Munich had to bear the unfortunate burden of Austrian occupation from 1704 to 1714. When the farmers rebelled, the ringleaders were arrested and hanged, drawn, and quartered on Marienplatz. Their heads were displayed on pikes at Isar Gate.

After the war, the Bavarian aristocracy was not especially sympathetic to the tribulations of the citizenry. The nobles set about building splendid little palaces for themselves, including the Preysing, the Erzbischöfliches (Archbishop's), and the Törring-Jettenbach Palais, strategically situated near the Prince Elector's Residenz.

Peace in an English Garden

The people of Munich grew ever more xenophobic after Hungarian hussars took over the city in 1742. They were dispatched by Empress Maria Theresa in retaliation for the Bavarian Prince Elector's opposition to Austro-Hungarian involvement in Germany.

In this atmosphere of hostility, Maximilian III Joseph (1727–1777) could not have been surprised when the Munich bourgeoisie resisted his efforts to establish a court monopoly on the manufacture of goods. All the royal manufacturers went bankrupt, with the exception of Nymphenburg porcelain, which thrives to this day. A brighter note was struck with the building of the delightful Cuvilliéstheater and the performance there by one Wolfgang Amadeus Mozart of his operas *The Abduction from the Seraglio, The Marriage of Figaro,* and *The Magic Flute.*

When Maximilian III Joseph, the last of the true Wittelsbach line, died in 1777, the succession fell to Karl Theodor, a member of the Mannheim branch of the family. He didn't want to leave Mannheim, he didn't like Munich, and Munich didn't like him. The people were starving; there was no bread. Instead of wheat, Karl Theodor sent in soldiers to suppress the angry populace.

It was Benjamin Thompson, an American, who suggested a solution to Karl Theodor's predicament. With the prince's blessing, Count Rumford (as he was subsequently known) provided schools and work to keep the unruly soldiers off the streets. He set up workshops and soup kitchens for the poor. (The potato-and-barley soup that was dispensed in them, served in Munich to this day, is known as *Rumfordsuppe.*)

In 1789, Rumford requisitioned a marshy wilderness on the outskirts of town and detailed the soldiers to drain it for development as a gigantic public park. The final result of Rumford's efforts, the Englischer Garten, is an enduring monument to American enterprise.

New Hopes, Ancient Dreams

While Munich was cultivating its garden, the rest of Europe was in a revolutionary uproar. In such circumstances, the city could not remain isolated for long. In 1800 it was occupied by the French troops of General Jean Victor Moreau, who established his headquarters in Nymphenburg Palace.

Napoleon himself came to town in 1805 for the marriage of his wife Josephine's son, Eugène de Beauharnais, to Princess Augusta of Bavaria. The journey to Munich did not inconvenience the emperor too much, as it was on the way to Austerlitz, where he was to fight the Russians and Austrians. Napoleon elevated Max IV Joseph from Prince Elector to King of Bavaria, and in exchange took a vast contingent of Bavarians on his Russian campaign of 1812, where he left 30,000 of them to die on the battlefield. Under pressure from the French, Max Joseph emancipated the Protestants of Munich, improved conditions for the Jews, and introduced a more moderate constitution.

Somehow, amid all the troubles of war and revolution, Munich managed to celebrate once again. Heeding the new spirit of the times, the royal court chose not to exclude the populace from the celebrations in honor of the marriage of Max Joseph's son, Ludwig, to Theresa of Saxony. On 17

The Nymphenburg Palace, where the Gallery of Beautiful Women contains portraits commissioned by Ludwig I.

October 1810, horseraces were organized, with great success. They developed into an annual event, now the Oktoberfest.

Munich itself was gradually expanding to the north and west into Maxvorstadt, a region that links the city center to Schwabing. The Graeco-Roman architecture of the Nationaltheater brought to the city the first signs of the Classical spirit that was to become the obsession of Ludwig I.

Born in Strasbourg, Ludwig (1786–1868) was determined to break the French stranglehold on German culture and to make Munich the leader of a new nationalist movement. During the Napoleonic occupation, the civic symbol of the Münchner Kindl had been replaced with an imperial lion; Ludwig made sure that the little monk was restored.

Familiar with the architecture of Rome and the Greek monuments of Sicily, Ludwig wanted to turn Munich into an "Athens-on-the-Isar." His first step was to move Bavaria's university from Landshut to Munich, where it was established along Ludwigstrasse in the Schwabing area first developed under his father's rule.

He built majestic Odeonsplatz with its Siegestor (Gate of Victory). The gate, which was badly scarred by bombs during World War II, has since become a symbol of defeat. Königsplatz, with its Greek Revival architecture, was the most complete realization of Ludwig's Classical aspirations. Typically, Ludwig himself laid the foundation stone for the Alte Pinakothek (the gallery designed to house the royal art collections) on 7 April 1826, the anniversary of the painter Raphael's birth.

A prodigious worker, rising before dawn each day to go to his office in the Residenz, the king gained some diversion from his sober duties by commissioning a series of portraits of the most beautiful young women of Munich. The collection hangs in the Schönheitengalerie (Gallery of Beautiful Women) at the Nymphenburg Palace. Included is his mistress, a dancer known as Lola Montez, with whom he fell in love when he was 60 and she 28. She was Ludwig's ruin. He made her the Countess von Landsfeld, to the horror both of his conservative ministers and the radical university students. In 1848, as revolution swept Europe, the students and the angry citizens of Munich forced Ludwig to deport Lola, and he abdicated in disgust. Ludwig's successor, Maximilian II (1811–1864), boosted Munich's cultural reputation thanks to his intimacy with illustrious thinkers such as the historian Leopold von Ranke, the philosopher Friedrich von Schelling, and the chemist Justus von Liebig.

End of a Dream

The last great king of Bavaria was the romantic king, Ludwig II (1845–1886), famous for his collaboration with

Richard Wagner. Under Ludwig's patronage, the composer staged in Munich the premières of his operas *Tristan und Isolde*, *Die Meistersinger von Nürnberg*, *Das Rhinegold*, and *Die Walküre*.

In the mundane world of 19th-century industrial expansion, Ludwig dreamt of making Munich the music capital of the world. He wanted to build a gigantic theater for his idol Wagner, a place where the composer could develop his concept of *Gesamtkunstwerk*—a synthesis of music, lyrics, and theater. But the banalities of state finances interfered and he was forced to relinquish the project to Bayreuth.

Ludwig acted out his fantasies in the eccentric fairy-tale palaces he built outside Munich—a medieval castle at Neuschwanstein, a beautiful French château at Linderhof, and a fanciful version of Versailles' Grand Trianon at Herrenchiemsee. Ironically, it was at a castle (the 16th-century Schloss Berg on Lake Starnberg) that Ludwig's life came to a sad and mysterious end. By 1886, Ludwig's wild behavior had persuaded the Bavarian government that he was mad, and a special commission declared him to be so. In consequence, the director of a mental asylum accompanied him to Schloss Berg and the two were later found drowned. It has never been determined whether their deaths were the result of murder or suicide.

Uncle Luitpold took over as regent (in place of Ludwig's brother, the insane King Otto). He presided over the grand *fin de siècle* artistic movement of the Jugendstil. This was followed a generation later by the Blaue Reiter school, which included Wassily Kandinsky, Paul Klee, and Franz Marc. Thomas Mann, Ranier Maria Rilke, Stefan George, and other writers moved to Schwabing. The artistic ferment also attracted a young painter from Vienna, an embittered man named Adolf Hitler.

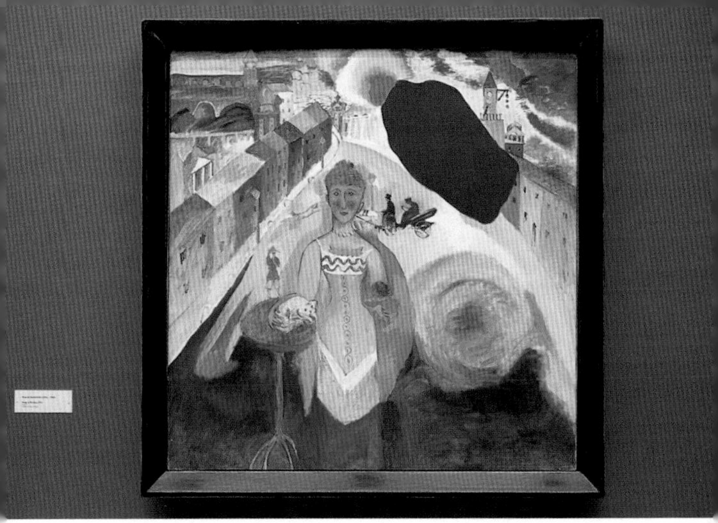

Lenbachhaus houses a number of paintings by Wassily Kandinsky, member of the esteemed Blaue Reiter school.

The Wittelsbach dynasty, along with others in Vienna and Berlin, ended in the disaster of World War I. Bavarians resented having been dragged into the European conflict by what they felt was Prussian belligerence, and a new social democratic movement gained support. In November 1918, with the war in its last days, Kurt Eisner led a march of workers and peasants from the Theresienwiese. En route, disaffected soldiers took control of their barracks and hoisted the red flag of revolution. The Bavarian Republic was declared in the Mathäser Bräuhaus (breweries traditionally being a favored spot for political action in Munich). The people invaded the Residenz and wandered around hooting for echoes in the vast galleries and ballrooms. Ludwig III, the last Wittelsbach king, fled in a car from the palace.

But the newly born republic of workers, peasants, and soldiers, modeled on the soviets created under the Russian revolution, was subject to violent attack from the conservative press and from private armies of troops (*Freikorps*) roaming the streets. Playing on Bavarian xenophobia, the right wing attacked Eisner as a Berliner and as a Jew. Just three months after the November revolution, Eisner was dead, shot down by a young aristocrat hoping to curry favor with an extreme right-wing club.

A group of "coffee-house anarchists" led by the writers Ernst Toller and Erich Mühsam took over briefly, but they were soon replaced by hard-line communists. After fierce and bloody fighting with the Freikorps, the Bavarian Red Army was defeated, and the short-lived independent republic of Bavaria was crushed. In the space of six months, Munich had known in breathtaking succession a monarchy, revolutionary socialism, moderate socialism, anarchy, communism and, finally, brutal counter-revolutionary oppression. Thus, a tolerant tradition was swept away and the city became a breeding ground for extremist political and paramilitary groups.

Hitler's Munich

Adolf Hitler had first been drawn to Munich by its cultural ambiance, but he remained immune to the innovative tendencies of the avant-garde. His own painting was stolidly academic and attracted no attention. He turned to the clamor of German nationalism, and a chance photograph taken at a rally on Odeonsplatz in August 1914 shows Hitler in the crowd, joyfully greeting news of the declaration of war.

He returned to Munich as a corporal in 1918. It was while working to re-educate soldiers in nationalistic, anti-Marxist ideas at the end of the Bavarian Republic that he joined the

Deutsche Arbeiter-Partei. By February 1920, he was able to address 2,000 members in the Hofbräuhaus. The association soon became known as the Nationalsozialistische Deutsche Arbeiter-Partei, or Nazi Party, and its symbol was the swastika. Armed storm troops of the party's Sturm-Abteilung (SA) broke up any opposition political meetings held in Munich.

At a January 1923 meeting Hitler said: "Either the Nazi Party is the German movement of the future, in which case no devil can stop it, or it isn't, in which case it deserves to be destroyed." Both proved true. By November, the party had 55,000 members and 15,000 storm troops. Hitler then felt strong enough to stage his famous Beer Hall Putsch.

This was intended as a first move in the campaign to force the Bavarian state government to cooperate in a Nazi march on Berlin. The putsch ended in a debacle on Odeonsplatz with Hitler being sent to prison, but not before he had turned the whole affair to his advantage.

Hitler ensured that his trial for treason became an indictment of his prosecutors as accomplices of the "November criminals" who, he said, had stabbed Germany in the back in 1918 with their anti-war movement. He became an instant hero. In prison at nearby Landsberg, Hitler was treated as an honored guest. He was not required to perform prison

Visitors to the Concentration Camp Museum study the map of the sobering locale.

work, but instead held political meetings and used his time to write *Mein Kampf.*

Hitler's career took him to Berlin, but the Nazis kept their party headquarters in Munich at the Brown House (named after the color of their shirts). Brighter spirits of the time, including whimsical comedian Karl Valentin and a fan of his, dramatist Bertolt Brecht, also made their home in Munich.

In 1935, Munich became known as the "Capital of the (Nazi) Movement." Its status at the vanguard was confirmed in June 1938, when the central synagogue was looted, presaging the *Kristallnacht* (Crystal Night) rampage five months later, when most of Germany's Jewish shops and houses of prayer were destroyed.

In September of that year, Munich also became a symbol of the ignominious appeasement of Britain and France. In

Beer, Bluff, and Bullets

The Beer Hall Putsch, which launched Hitler's national career, was staged in the Bürgerbräukeller. It gave a foretaste of the crazy melodrama, bluff, and shameless gall he was later to exhibit on the world scene.

With the Bavarian minister Gustav von Kahr about to speak, Hitler burst into the crowded room, smashed a beer mug to the floor, and pushed forward at the head of his storm troops, brandishing a pistol. In the pandemonium, he jumped on a table and fired a shot into the ceiling. "National revolution has broken out!" he yelled. "Farce! South America!" was the response from a few wags, who were promptly beaten up. The new Hitler style of politics had indisputably arrived. Today the Bürgerbräukeller has been replaced by the Hilton City Hotel; there is no plaque commemorating the putsch.

Munich's Führerbau, a meeting took place between prime ministers Neville Chamberlain and Edouard Daladier, during which they negotiated the dismemberment of Czechoslovakia with Hitler and Mussolini. Later, Chamberlain obtained a signed piece of paper from the Führer, which he wishfully waved at the British people as a guarantee of "peace in our time."

War and Peace

One spark of resistance from wartime Munich came when two students, Hans and Sophie Scholl, courageously distributed anti-Hitler "White Rose" leaflets. But brother and sister were betrayed and executed.

World War II brought 71 air raids to the city, killing 6,000 and wounding 16,000. Bombardments were most intense in 1944, heavily damaging the Frauenkirche, St. Peter's, and St. Michael's churches and large parts of the Residenz and Alte Pinakothek. The Brown House was destroyed but, ironically, the majority of Hitler's other buildings were left intact.

The postwar reconstruction was a triumph of hard work and fiercely loyal attachment to the great traditions of Munich's past. Monuments, palaces, and churches were all restored with meticulous care. Traditionally open to the arts and to good living in general, Munich expanded and became Germany's third-largest city (total population 1,316,000), welcoming many Berliners and refugees from the former eastern territories.

The city has continued to build on its international reputation as a city of culture, with a year-round program of performing-arts productions, including concerts and open-air opera in the beautiful surroundings of the great palaces and monuments. Visitors to Munich can be sure of a taste of good living, Bavarian-style.

HISTORICAL LANDMARKS

Eighth c.	Small settlement of Benedictine monks gives the site its name, Ze den Munichen.
1158	Henry the Lion sets up toll station for the passage of salt from Salzburg.
1180	Emperor Barbarossa takes Munich from Henry and hands city over to the Wittelsbach family.
1328	Duke Ludwig IV becomes Holy Roman Emperor —court established in Munich.
1348	Black Death brings devastation to Munich.
15th c.	Prosperous period—Munich established as transit point for trade from Venice.
1632	Swedish armies invade Munich during the Thirty Years' War; Munich devastated by plague.
1638	Mariensäule set up on Marienplatz.
1704–1714	Austrian occupation of Munich.
1742	Hungarian hussars take over the city.
1789	American Benjamin Thompson develops today's Englischer Garten as a public park.
1805	Napoleon visits Munich.
1806	Napoleon raises Bavaria to status of Kingdom.
1845	Bavarian King Ludwig II is born.
1886	Ludwig II found drowned at Schloss Berg.
1918	The Bavarian Republic declared. Ludwig III flees.
1920	Adolph Hitler addresses the Deutsche Arbeiter-Partei at the Hofbräuhaus.
1923	Hitler stages his famous "Beer Hall Putsch."
1935	Munich named Capital of the Nazi Movement.
1939-1945	World War II: 71 air raids on the city, killing 6,000 and wounding 16,000.
1972	Munich hosts the Summer Olympic Games.
1985	Opening of the Gasteig arts complex.
1992	Opening of the new airport, Flughafen München Franz Josef Strauss.
1998	Munich Trade Fair, Messe München International, opens new grounds.

WHERE TO GO

Munich has two enormous assets as far as the visitor is concerned. First, a large majority of the city's museums, monuments, palaces, and churches are concentrated in the Innenstadt (inner city), which makes Munich a great town for walking. Second, the superb public transport system, which incorporates buses, trams, underground (*U-Bahn*), and surface trains (*S-Bahn*), brings all the other sights within easy reach.

Rather than dealing with the complicated business of driving your car around town, it would be wisest to find a parking spot on the outskirts of town (parking is almost impossible in the center) and save the car for excursions. If you walk wherever you can, you'll see more of the town's bustling street life and drop in more easily at the outdoor cafés. You'll be able to indulge in the pleasure of discovering Munich's unexpected courtyard vistas and its hidden alleyways. You'll also happen upon numerous little bars and shops tucked away in odd corners that you would completely miss in a car.

So, apart from the section devoted to excursions, Munich is presented here in a series of walks.

INNENSTADT

Munich long ago expanded beyond the confines of its medieval boundaries, and the old city wall has now disappeared. However, the remains of three gates survive to indicate the perimeter of the inner city—Isartor, Karlstor, and Sendlinger Tor—as well as Odeonsplatz, a rendezvous for salt traders setting off in the 14th century for northern Germany. Ever since Munich's earliest beginnings, however, Marienplatz has been at the heart of it all.

Marienplatz to Theatinerstrasse

Until the middle of the 19th century, **Marienplatz** was the place where the wheat market was held. The square was the obvious site for the town hall, and was the place where criminals were hanged. Marienplatz was also the scene of the most extravagant wedding Munich has ever seen—that of Duke Wilhelm V to Renata of Lorraine in 1568. It was the inevitable choice for the central junction of the U-Bahn and S-Bahn system in 1972.

Graced with its tubs of flowers and outdoor cafés, Marienplatz today forms part of an attractive pedestrian zone. It is the home of the **Mariensäule** (Column of the Virgin Mary), erected in 1638 by Maximilian I in gratitude for the town's deliverance from the Plague after its defeat by the Swedes during the Thirty Years' War. At the base of the column are a basilisk, dragon, serpent, and lion—which represent plague, hunger, heresy, and war—each being vanquished by heroic child-angels. On the top of the monument is the majestic figure of Mary, who watches over Munich. Holding Jesus in her left arm and a sceptre in her right, she is a reminder of Munich's religious foundation. The square also contains the partially reconstructed 19th-century Fischbrunnen monument. Young butchers used to leap into the bronze fountain at the end of their apprenticeship, but today the tradition is kept up only by Fasching (carnival) revelers or happy soccer fans.

Standing at the eastern end of Marienplatz is the almost too picturesque **Altes Rathaus** (Old Town Hall), an example of Munich's efforts to reconstruct, rather than replace, the remnants of its venerable history. The dove-gray façade, amber-tiled steeple, and graceful little spires of this Gothic-style edifice capture the spirit of the 15th-century original designed by Jörg von Halsbach (also called Jörg Ganghofer), though it

Munich Highlights

(See also Museum and Art Gallery Highlights on page 56)

Asamkirche, Sendlinger Strasse 62; *U-bahn 1, 3, 6 Sendlinger Tor.* The idiosyncratic Church of St. Johann Nepomuk, with flamboyant rococo façade and interior. (See page 45)

Bavaria Film Studios, Bavariafilmplatz 7, Geiselgasteig, Tel. (089) 64 992 304; web site <www.bavaria-film.de>; *U-bahn 1, 2 to Silberhornstraße, then Tram 25.* Tours take place daily from 9am–4pm 1 Mar–31 Oct. Stunt shows are staged daily at 11:30am and 12:30pm.On holidays and weekends there is an additional show at 2pm. Entry fee—DM15 adults, DM5 children.

Englischer Garten: *U-bahn Giselastraße or Münchener Freiheit.* Beautiful park along the River Isar. Don't miss the city's largest beer garden next to the Chinese Tower. (See page 52)

Frauenkirche: one of Munich's most identifiable landmarks. Open Mon–Sat 10am–5pm. DM4 adults, DM2 children. (See page 33)

Hofbräuhaus, Platzl, Tel. (089) 221 676. Don't miss this famous beer hall for dinner or just for some after-dinner entertainment. (See page 39)

Marienplatz: the heart of Munich. Go at 11am for the 43-bell Glockenspiel of the Neues Rathaus. (see page 30)

Nymphenburg Palace, Tel. (089) 17908-0; *Tram 12, bus 21.* A beautiful building with wonderful gardens and museums. Open daily except Mon, 9am–12:30pm and 1:30–5pm April–Sept, and 10am–12:30pm and 1:30–4pm Oct–Mar. DM11 adults, DM8 children. (See page 71)

Residenz, Max-Joseph Platz, Tel. (089) 290 671; *U-bahn 3, 4, 5, 6 Odeonsplatz, tram 19.* Formerly the residence of the Wittelsbachs, it is now an incredible museum. Open daily (except Mon), 10am–4:30pm. DM7 adults, children 14 and under free. (See page 42)

St. Peter's: the city's oldest church, dating before 1158. Make the long climb to the top for a breathtaking view. Open 9am–6pm Mon–Sat and 10am–6pm Sundays and holidays. Entry fee DM2.50, children DM0.50. (See page 37)

Viktualienmarkt: just south of the Marienplatz, this market is one of the most colorful areas of Munich. (See page 45) isn't an exact replica. In any case, with the addition over the centuries of a Baroque, onion-shaped cupola and then a too-conscientious "regothification," the building that was destroyed by Allied bombs was probably further from the original than what you see today.

Apart from a banquet hall on an upper floor, the Altes Rathaus fulfills a mainly decorative function. The daily business of city government takes place at the **Neues Rathaus** (New Town Hall) on the northern side of Marienplatz. This is a classic example of 19th-century Neo-Gothic architecture: proud and self-assertive, its façade is elaborately decorated with the statues of kings, princes and dukes, saints, allegorical figures, and characters from the folklore of Munich. The tower is around 80 m (260 ft) high. Its main attraction, apart from the splendid view (if you want to take the elevator to the top) is the 43-bell Glockenspiel (carillon) which puts on a show daily at 11am. Two groups of figures appear, one group re-enacting the tournament held during the wedding of Duke Wilhelm V and Renata of Lorraine and the other, underneath, re-creating the cooper's dance (*Schäfflertanz*), which was performed to exorcize the plague of

The illuminated Altes Rathaus lights up the Marienplatz at night.

1517. In the evening, at 9pm, a night watchman with lantern blows his horn and an angel of peace blesses the little Munich monk (Münchner Kindl).

Now go along Weinstrasse (around the corner at the west end of the Neues Rathaus) and left along Sporerstrasse to the **Frauenkirche.** Its full title is Domkirche zu Unserer Lieben Frau (Cathedral Church of Our Lady). This building, perhaps more than any other, symbolizes Munich, its gold-tipped, bulbous domes on twin brick towers dominating the skyline. The church, an austere, unadorned Gothic structure, was built between 1468 and 1488 by Jörg von Halsbach. The Italian Renaissance domes are an addition of 1524. After extensive reconstruction work on the exterior, the church is now once again open daily.

The stark interior was reconstructed from the rubble of World War II bombardments, a truly heroic work of restoration. The original Gothic windows in the choir, stored in safety during the war, give an impression of the church's former glory. Fine sculptures of the Apostles and Prophets also escaped destruction and adorn the choir as before. They were created by Erasmus Grasser in 1502. An admirable altarpiece of 1483 by Friedrich Pacher, the *Baptism of Christ*, hangs in the north chapel. It is flanked by Jan Polack's panels depicting Jesus on the Mount of Olives and his arrest, crucifixion, and burial. Notice, too, the 17th-century funerary monument of Emperor Ludwig the Bavarian, who died in 1347. Just outside the church, the granite fountain in Frauenplatz strikes a modern note. A waterfall plays, and stones are set out in the shape of an amphitheater to provide seating.

Augustinerstrasse, west of the square, leads to Neuhauser Strasse and what was once the church of the Augustinians. The building became a customs house in the time of

Say, "Cheese!" A boar statue stands guard at the Hunting and Fishing Museum.

Napoleon and then, in 1966, a museum of hunting and fishing, the Deutsches Jagd- und Fischereimuseum. Proclaimed by a wild boar in bronze, the collection will fascinate hunters, anglers, and children alike.

Go farther along pedestrian-zoned Neuhauser Strasse to the 16th-century **St. Michael's,** an Italian Renaissance church with Baroque overtones (the first of its kind in Germany), largely designed by the Dutch architect Friedrich Sustris. St. Michael's epitomizes the combative spirit of the Counter-Reformation, and it is fitting that the Wittelsbach dukes and German emperors, the secular defenders of the faith, are depicted on the gabled façade. Above the entrance, third figure from the right, stands the church's patron, Duke Wilhelm V (with a scale model of St. Michael's Church in his hand). Il Gesù, in Rome, was the inspiration for the Baroque interior of St. Michael's, which surpasses the former in its masterful lighting.

Karlstor, a city gate dating from the 14th century, links Neuhauser Strasse to the busy Karlsplatz, which is popularly known as the Stachus after an innkeeper named Eustachius Föderl. The **Stachus** conceals a veritable city of underground shops, which extends from the exit of the U- and S-

Bahn station. Walk north to Lenbachplatz and you'll find the city's loveliest fountain, the **Wittelsbacher Brunnen,** which was built in Neo-Baroque style by Adolf von Hildebrand at the end of the 19th century.

Pacellistrasse, to the east of Lenbachplatz, takes you past the Baroque façade of the **Dreifaltigkeitskirche** (Trinity Church). In 1704 a young girl, Anna Maria Lindmayr, dreamt that Munich would be invaded and destroyed unless a new church were constructed. Sure enough, the next year, during the War of the Spanish Succession, Austrian soldiers arrived. Although work on the Dreifaltigkeitskirche did not begin until 1711, the town was saved from destruction.

Finding Your Way...

Here are some terms that may help you when traveling in Bavaria (the ß symbol should be read as ss):

Allee	boulevard
Bahnhof	railway station
Brücke	bridge
Brunnen	fountain
Burg	castle, fortress
Dom	cathedral
Gasse	alley
Kirche	church
Markt	market
Rathaus	town hall
Platz	square
Schloß	castle, palace
See	lake
Stift	monastery
Straße/Strasse	street
Ufer	river bank
Weg	path, way

Promenadeplatz is noted for the elegance of Palais Montgelas. This Neo-Classical building today forms part of the upscale Bayerischer Hof hotel, where you might like to refresh yourself with a drink at the bar.

Continue north along Kardinal-Faulhaber-Strasse past the Palais Porcia, one of Munich's first Baroque palaces, now a bank, to the **Erzbischöfliches Palais** (Archbishop's Palace) at number 7, a triumph of Rococo harmony with especially fine stucco work. Originally known as Palais Holnstein, it's the only 18th-century palace built by François de Cuvilliés (see page 43) to have survived intact to the present day.

A good place to end your walk is in the shopping arcades of Theatinerstrasse and spoil yourself in a *Konditorei*, a café specializing in pastries and coffee.

Isartorplatz to Platzl

The sturdy Isartor, in its restored form, is the only city gate that retains its original 14th-century dimensions. Put up in the days when the Bavarian Duke Ludwig IV was Holy Roman Emperor, a later fresco of 1835 on the gate shows the emperor returning triumphantly from victory over the Hapsburgs. The Isartor now serves as a rather overgrown traffic island, but one of the towers houses a roof-top café and the Valentin-Museum, devoted to the famous cabaret comic of 1920s Munich, Karl Valentin (see box, page 50).

From Isartor, go along Tal, a shopping street that takes you to **Heiliggeistkirche** (Church of the Holy Spirit). This 14th-century Gothic structure was extensively altered to suit the Baroque tastes of the 1720s. The two styles come together perfectly in the **Marienaltar**—a lovely wooden sculpture of 1450, the *Hammerthaler Muttergottes* (Hammerthal Mother of God) originally from the Lake Tegernsee monastery, set in an opulent gilded Baroque framework. The reconstructed high altar preserves a fine pair of *Adoring Angels* from 1730 by Johann Georg Greiff.

West of Heiliggeistkirche, with an entrance on Rindermarkt, is **St. Peter's,** the oldest church in Munich, dating from before the foundation of the city itself in 1158. The original structure gave way to a building in the Romanesque style, succeeded in time by a Gothic church that boasted a twin-steepled tower. Everything but the tower was destroyed in the great fire of 1327, and a new Gothic structure went up. This was remodeled along Renaissance lines in the 17th century, and a new tower with a single steeple was created. Destroyed in the war, St. Peter's has been faithfully reconstructed, down to the asymmetrically placed clocks on the tower. (Follow the crowd to the top for a stunning view of the inner city.)

The oldest church in Munich, St. Peter's is filled with artistic and architectural marvels.

The crowning piece of the light, bright interior is the **high altar** glorifying Peter and the fathers of the Church. It was restored from the remnants of the 18th-century original, inspired by Bernini's altar for St. Peter's in Rome. Egid Quirin Asam (see page 44) was the designer of the ensemble, incorporating Erasmus Grasser's *St. Peter*. The gilded

A 12-sided temple dedicated to Diana forms the centerpiece of the Hofgarten.

wood figures of the Church fathers are the masterly work of Egid Quirin.

Leading up to the altar are splendid Rococo choir stalls. You'll also see five of Jan Polack's Late Gothic paintings that once adorned the altar. The paintings show Peter healing the lame, enthroned, at sea, in prison, and on the cross. Also from the Late Gothic period is the Schrenk-Altar, a fine early 15th-century sandstone relief of the Crucifixion and the Day of Judgment.

Coming out, duck along little Burgstrasse past the Altes Rathaus. Stop at number 5 to admire the **Weinstadl,** one of only a few Gothic houses still left in Munich, once the home of the town clerk and now a restaurant. Built in about 1550, it has a neatly restored, leafy courtyard and a staircase tower.

The **Alter Hof** is a miracle of inner-city tranquillity. The peaceful, tree-shaded square presents an exquisite panorama of medieval buildings. The reconstructed Burgtor (City Gate) nearby, and quaint little Affenturm (Monkey Tower)—incorporated in the west wing—recapture the atmosphere of the Wittelsbachs' first Munich residence as it was in the 15th century. The splendid heraldic painting on the tower came to light in the 1960s.

The Hof was originally built around 1255 on what was then the northeast corner of town, in defense against foreign invaders as well as the city's own unruly burghers. It was superseded by the more massive Residenz. The buildings suffered more at the hands of 19th-century urban developers than during the 20th-century bombing, but the careful reconstruction of the surviving south and west wings gives an idea of their former grandeur.

Turn right on Pfisterstrasse to Platzl (Little Square), the site of a building of no great architectural distinction but, nevertheless, the most publicized monument in Munich, the **Hofbräuhaus** beer hall. Duke Wilhelm V founded a brewery in the Alter Hof in 1589 to avoid paying the high prices for imported beer from Hanover. Beer has always been just as much an aristocratic as a plebeian drink in Bavaria. It replaced wine as the staple alcoholic beverage after the Bavarian vineyards were destroyed by the cruel winters of the 13th and 14th centuries, making way for the sturdier hop and barley crops.

The brewery was first established in the royal bath house, and moved to the more spacious quarters on Platzl in 1644. The Hofbräuhaus itself was built in 1896, after the brewery was transferred to the other side of the River Isar. It soon became the most prestigious of Munich's many political beer-hall arenas. In fact, in November 1921, Hitler's storm troops first gained notoriety in what became known as the "*Schlacht im Hofbräuhaus*" (Battle of the Hofbräuhaus). Today, the huge beer hall, with its long tables and oom-pah-pah music, is a magnet for tourists. Don't be surprised to see dogs sitting with their owners in the Hofbräuhaus or in any other city restaurants—it's perfectly acceptable here in Munich.

Odeonsplatz to Maximilianstrasse

Odeonsplatz joins the inner city to Schwabing and the university. At this spot Ludwig I opened up the overcrowded heart of town to the more airy Vorstadt, Schwabing then being no more than a suburb.

This particularly airy and "liberating" walk begins in the Italian Renaissance-style Hofgarten (Court Garden), now restored and replanted with the chestnut trees, flower beds, and fountains specified in the original 17th-century plan. In the center stands a 12-sided temple dedicated to Diana, topped by a bronze statue of Bavaria. The arcades that line the garden house art galleries and cafés, and are decorated with frescoes of historic scenes that feature the Wittelsbachs. To the north (Galeriestrasse 4) is a fascinating **Theatermuseum,** worth visiting for the display of famous set designs from Munich's rich theatrical past.

Now turn and look southwest across the Hofgarten to capture the delightful vista that helps to give Munich its peculiarly Mediterranean flavor—the twin towers and dome of the splendid **Theatinerkirche.** This Italian Baroque church was built between 1663 and 1688 by two Italian architects, Agostino Barelli and Enrico Zuccalli. The façade was completed later by Cuvilliés.

Perhaps because the church was built to celebrate the birth of a baby boy to Princess Henriette Adelaide, a feeling of jubilation animates its rich decoration—with sprigs of ornamental vines, acanthus leaves and rosettes in the most spirited Italian Baroque style, and wonderful gray-and-white stucco embellishments in the cupola. Notice, as well, the triumphant pulpit, the high altar (a copy of one destroyed by bombs) and, to the left, the Kajetan altar. This last was dedicated to St. Kajetan, founder of the Theatine

Order commemorated in the church's title.

Just across the street, facing Odeonsplatz, is the **Feldherrnhalle** (Hall of the Generals), a 19th-century monument to a number of Bavarian military leaders, including the Belgian-born Count Johann Tilly (a hero in the Thirty Years' War) and Prince Karl-Philipp von Wrede, who achieved victory over the French in 1814. Less gloriously, it was the rendezvous for Nazi storm troops in Hitler's unsuccessful putsch of 1923, and was subsequently a focus for marches commemorating the event. Reinforcing the Italian atmosphere of the area, though with less of a light touch, the building is modeled after the Late Gothic Loggia dei Lanzi in Florence.

The Feldherrnhalle (Hall of the Generals) pays tribute to many great warriors.

Nearby, in Residenzstrasse, is **Preysing-Palais,** the most lavishly ornamented private Rococo palace in Munich. Begun in 1723 by Joseph Effner, the Residenzstrasse façade was the only part to survive World War II, but the restoration of other parts was masterful. Take a look inside at the imposing ceremonial staircase.

At the other end of the street lies another jewel of 18th-century architecture, formerly the **Hauptpostamt,** or Main Post

Max-Joseph is memorialized with this statue that sits before the Nationaltheater.

Office, and originally the Palais Törring-Jettenbach. The northern façade was given a face-lift in the 19th century to fit in with the Classical demands of the Residenz and Nationaltheater on Maximilianstrasse. But the original Baroque door-way can be seen inside. Completely rebuilt in 1963, the **Nationaltheater** is a faithful copy of the original building of 1818, a Greek-temple design by Karl von Fischer.

Max-Joseph-Platz is named after the king whose statue sits in the center. The fourth Max-Joseph of the Wittelsbach dynasty and the first, thanks to Napoleon, to be king, wanted what he considered to be a more dignified standing pose. Unfortunately, he died before the statue was completed, so his son Ludwig I accepted the seated version.

The statue was put alongside the greatest monument of Max-Joseph's family, the Wittelsbach **Residenz.** In 1385 the citizenry revolted, driving the dukes to construct safer lodgings than the Alter Hof (see page 38). More than five centuries later, in 1918, another group of rebellious citizens pounded on the Residenz doors during the revolution that resulted in the short-lived Bavarian Republic. The Wittelsbachs had to move out once again, and this time it was for good.

Many of the Bavarian dukes and kings were passionate art collectors and keen builders. The Residenz, now a museum, shows just how powerful and immensely wealthy the proud Bavarian principality grew to be. To view the exterior, enter via Residenzstrasse and walk through the seven courtyards to the Cuvilliéstheater (within the Residenz but not included on museum tours).

The splendid **Cuvilliéstheater,** or Altes Residenztheater, is one of the most enchanting playhouses in the world. Its architect François de Cuvilliés was a dwarf from the Spanish Netherlands. The theater is tiny, seating only 450. But its sense of festive intimacy turns every performance into a cozy gala. The four-tiered, horseshoe-shaped auditorium basks in gilded Rococo décor with hosts of Greek nymphs, gods and goddesses, and, with marvelous incongruity, an American Indian girl with her bow and arrows. The acoustics are warm and golden—totally suited to the Mozart works that have been played here for the past 200 years.

The Cuvilliéstheater owes its existence to planning and foresight. In 1943, its stucco ornamentation and sculptures were dismantled. Some 30,000 pieces were carried away and stored in the vaults of various castles around Munich. Only six weeks later the theater was gutted by fire bombs. However, fifteen years elapsed before all the pieces were brought out of hiding and reassembled.

Sendlinger Tor to Viktualienmarkt

The walk from Sendlinger Tor takes you through the busy shopping area of Sendlinger Strasse, and past the municipal museum to the open-air market next to St. Peter's church. Only two hexagonal towers remain from the 14th-century **Sendlinger Tor** (City Gate).

Facing northeast, follow the left fork along Sendlinger Strasse to **Asamhaus** (number 61), where Egid Quirin Asam, a master sculptor and architect of the 18th century, lived. He was assisted in the decoration of the building by his brother, Cosmas Damian, who specialized in fresco painting. The ornate forenames of the brothers are suited to the rich Baroque style favored by the two.

Stand on the opposite side of Sendlinger Strasse and look at the marvelously intricate façade of the house, built in 1733. Secure in their Catholic faith, the Asam brothers happily mixed pagan and Christian figures in their decorative schemes. Just below the roof to the right (directly above the doorway) you'll see a representation in stucco of heaven and the monogram of Christ. Below that appears the seated figure of Mary. To the left is a vine-bedecked Olympus, and Apollo is accompanied by the triumphant gods of Fame and Fortune. Pegasus, the flying horse, leaps up to them while, lower down, a riot of nymphs and satyrs dance around the Muses of painting, sculpture, and architecture. The original doorway, on which are depicted scenes from the Old and New Testaments, is now displayed in

Viktualienmarkt, Munich's central food market—in business since 1807.

the Bavarian National Museum (see page 54). Enormous diligence and ingenuity marks the decoration of Asamhaus. It also confirms the brothers' lighthearted devotion to the good life and to their religion.

The ultimate demonstration of this can be seen next door in the Asams' private church of St. Johann Nepomuk, which was originally linked to Egid Quirin's house. This church, popularly known as **Asamkirche,** was completed in 1746. Built at Egid Quirin's own expense, the church's design was free from the constraints of a patron's demands. The result is a subjective celebration of faith and life.

Its variegated marble façade serves as a street-altar for the passers-by on busy Sendlinger Strasse. The church incorporates unhewn rocks originally intended for a fountain; a statue of John of Nepomuk, a Bohemian saint popular in the 18th century, stands over the porch. Inside, the **high altar** leads the eye up to a large Crucifixion dominated by a representation of God the Father wearing the papal crown.

The impressive four-story **Altes Hackerhaus** is on the corner of Hackenstrasse. This rare surviving example of a private dwelling in the Classical style has a succession of nine Doric, Ionic, and Corinthian pillars running along each façade, and beautiful, historic living rooms. Go farther along Hackenstrasse to the corner of Hotterstrasse, where Munich's oldest operating tavern, Gaststätte zur Hundskugel, has been serving beer since 1440.

If you double back across Sendlinger Strasse, you'll find St-Jakobs-Platz and the **Münchner Stadtmuseum** (Municipal Museum; see page 66). To the east of this fascinating museum lies one of the most colorful locations in Munich and a magnet for all who love food, the **Viktualienmarkt.** The city's central food market has been doing business here since 1807. Stroll around the enticing stalls with their myriad cheeses and exotic spices, breads, and meats. The cornucopia of vegetables and fruit prove better than anything else that Munich is a crossroads of northern and southern Europe, and a gateway to the East as well.

The cheerful atmosphere of the market makes it the perfect place for annual performances of the Marketwomen's Dance, held on Shrove Tuesday. It's also the scene of a number of lively celebrations around the flower-bedecked maypole.

AROUND KONIGSPLATZ

To the northwest of the inner city, beyond the Alter Botanischer Garten, **Königsplatz** represents a convergence of the noblest and basest aspirations arising from the past several hundred years of Munich's history. When Ludwig I was still crown prince, he visualized the square as a second Acropolis, a vast open space surrounded by Classical temples. There was no particular reason for the choice of this site (no junction of roads, for example). Ludwig simply overrode the customary demands of urban planning, and soon had men working on widening the stately Brienner Strasse, the street that took the royal family from the Residenz to Nymphenburg Palace.

With Leo von Klenze working as his architect, Ludwig turned the square into a grass-covered, tree-lined haven of tranquillity. A hundred years later, Hitler cut down the trees and paved over the grass for the troops and armored cars of his military parades. (The pompous Nazi **Ehrentempel,** or Temple of Honor, which stood at the eastern end of the square, was deliberately blown up by the Allied military engineers in 1945.) Today, at last, Königsplatz is returning to its original serenity, and the pastoral greenery is back.

The U-Bahn station brings you out beside the **Propyläen** (Propylaeum), modeled after the entranceway to the Acropolis in Athens. Unlike the original entranceway, this splendid

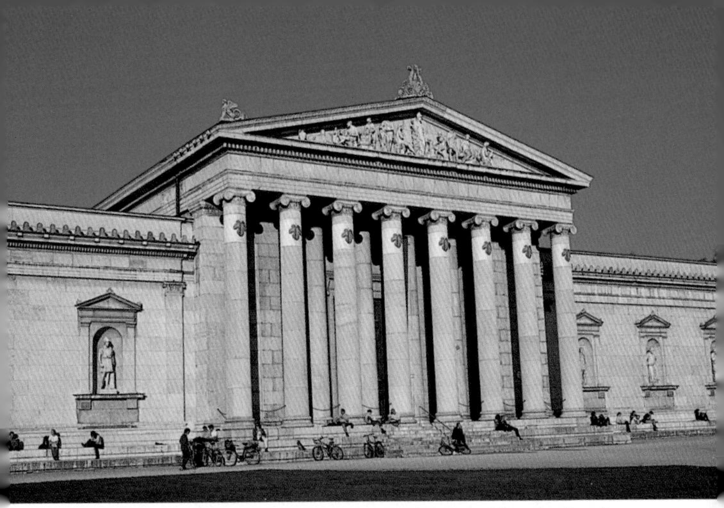

The Glyptothek, erected in 1807, is said to be the first building constructed for use as a public museum.

monument to Ludwig's sublime imperviousness to functional considerations does not lead anywhere, for it closes off Königsplatz rather than providing access to the square. Despite the Doric columns, it's not even authentically Greek, since the central "gateway" is flanked by two Egyptian-style pylons, or towers. The friezes that decorate them show the Wittelsbachs' special attachment to all things Greek: representations of the Greek war of liberation from the Turks, and of the Greek people paying homage to Ludwig's son Otto when he was made their king in 1832.

Before visiting the monuments on Königsplatz, continue walking past the Propyläen up to **Lenbachhaus** on Luisenstrasse. This elegant ochre-colored villa, constructed in the 1880s and based on the style of Renaissance Florence, was rebuilt after World War II. Franz von Lenbach, a wealthy academic painter highly regarded among the German aristocracy, built himself this showy palace with the fortune he accumulated from his art. Today the villa houses the excellent **Lenbachhaus und Kuntsbau Städtische Galerie** of 19th- and 20th-century art (see page 65). Coffee is served on the terrace or in the pleasant garden, and there is a little park just opposite in which you can play open-air chess on giant stone boards.

Situated on the south side of Königsplatz is the **Staatliche Antikensammlungen** (Classical Art Collections), which seems rather clumsily designed, with its Corinthian columns set on an excessively elevated pedestal. Just across the square stands the companion building, the **Glyptothek** (Sculpture Museum; see page 64). It was designed in 1815 by von Klenze to display Ludwig I's large collection of

Contemplating the masters at Alte Pinakothek, yet another venerable art institution commissioned by Ludwig I.

Greek and Roman sculpture, and was the first building to be planned and constructed for use as a public museum.

Cross over Gabelsberger Strasse to another venerable art institution, the **Alte Pinakothek.** Ludwig commissioned von Klenze to provide a design for a monumental museum in the style of an Italian Renaissance palace (see page 55). Reconstruction in 1958 preserved the spacious layout of galleries and cabinets and introduced some excellent lighting.

North of nearby Theresienstrasse is situated the strikingly modern **Neue Pinakothek** building, opened to the public in 1981. The work of Alexander von Branca, the elegant gray sandstone and granite structure replaces the original building destroyed in World War II. Extensive skylights provide superb natural lighting. The style of the architecture is a break with the Alte Pinakothek's Classical traditions, but it achieves a total harmony nonetheless. A third museum, Pinakothek der Moderne, scheduled to open in 2002, will display art of the 21st century. (For a description of Munich's museums, see pages 55–71.)

Two surviving examples of Hitler's architectural contribution to the city, at the east end of Königsplatz, are known as Führer's Buildings (*Führerbauten*). At Arcisstrasse 12, now housing a music academy (*Musikhochschule*), Hitler received Chamberlain and Daladier, the British and French prime ministers that accepted the infamous Munich agreement of 1938 (see page 26). Meiserstrasse 10 today is home to some of Germany's most important archaeological and art-historical institutions, but it was built in 1933 as an administrative center for the Nazi Party. These grim, bunker-like blocks, designed by Paul Ludwig Troost under the obsessive supervision of Hitler himself, ironically survived the American bombardments that severely damaged the historic Glyptothek and Staatliche Antikensammlungen.

Rather than finish the walk on this somber note, continue down Meiserstrasse to the **Alter Botanischer Garten.** Although the town's major botanical garden has now been transferred to Nymphenburg Palace (see page 71), the lawns here still make for a pleasant stroll. Take a seat by the Neptune Fountain and look over the trees for a view of the two cupolas of the Frauenkirche. It's amazing to think that the people of Munich found time to lay out this lovely, tranquil spot right in the middle of the Napoleonic Wars.

☛ SCHWABING

The Schwabing district is one of a select group of places—including Chelsea in London, Montparnasse in Paris, and Greenwich Village in New York—that have been described as "not so much a place as a state of mind."

Begin your walk symbolically (Munich loves symbols) at the Siegestor (Victory Gate), which marks the southern boundary of Schwabing. This triumphal arch was designed for Ludwig I as a monument to the Bavarian army. In 1944 the arch was badly damaged, and in 1958 only partially restored, leaving the scars of war and a new inscription on

Valentin's Day

Although little known outside Germany, Karl Valentin was regarded by connoisseurs as a comic genius equal to Charlie Chaplin. While resident in Munich in the early twenties, dramatist Bertolt Brecht went almost every night to watch Valentin's portrayal of the clownish, working-class characters of peasant origin who were so peculiar to the city.

Valentin quickly attracted the attention of Schwabing's artists and intellectuals, who loved his insane, surreal logic. One of his most celebrated sketches portrayed an attempt to house birds in an aquarium and fish in a bird-cage.

the south side: "Dem Sieg geweiht, im Krieg zerstört, zum Frieden mahnend" ("Dedicated to victory, destroyed in war, exhorting to peace"). More than any other part of Munich, Schwabing epitomizes a break with military traditions.

Walk to the entrance of the University and visit the little square named Geschwister-Scholl-Platz, in memory of the brother and sister who died in the struggle against Hitler (see page 27). Across the street is St. Ludwig's, a Neo-Romanesque church noted for the gigantic fresco of the *Last Judgement* in the choir, by Peter Cornelius (1836). After Michelangelo's in the Sistine Chapel, it's the world's second-largest fresco, measuring 18 m (60 ft) by 11 m (37 ft).

At night the bohemian spirit of Schwabing animates wide and breezy **Leopoldstrasse,** beginning north of Siegestor. The great writers and artists that frequented the street in the past may have disappeared, but the art galleries and cafés are still going strong, and there is an underlying sense of excitement as you stroll along what is jokingly referred to as Boulevard Leopold. Having provided a focus for the avant-garde of Jugendstil and the Blaue Reiter, Schwabing now serves as the meeting place for the talents of the new German cinema. You may well catch a glimpse of the latest popular directors or actors, or at least those aspiring to stardom.

Once you come upon Münchener Freiheit, a road junction and U-Bahn stop, follow Feilitzschstrasse to **Wedekindplatz,** a center of theater, cabaret, and café life reminiscent of the golden past. Continue on to Werneckstrasse and to **Suresnes-Schlösschen** (or the Little Château), which is now the Catholic Academy. It was built in 1718 for Prince Elector Max Emmanuel as a reminder of the ten happy years he spent at the French château of the same name during the War of the Spanish Succession. It was remodeled several times in the 19th century; some of the stucco work of the original Baroque structure can still be seen.

ENGLISCHER GARTEN AREA

From Schwabing, head east to the lovely **Englischer Garten.** Opened in 1793, the park was the brainchild of an American-born adventurer who had sided with the British in the American Revolution. Better known to the Bavarians as Count Rumford (see page 18), Benjamin Thompson drew his inspiration from the famous English landscape gardeners Capability Brown and William Chambers. In fact, the Chinesischer Turm (Chinese Tower), a decorative pagoda that functions as a bandstand in the popular beer garden, owes a great deal to Chambers' Cantonese Pagoda in London's Kew Gardens.

Rumford and his German associate Ludwig von Sckell broke with the French tradition, favored by the Bavarian aristocracy, of gardens with geometric avenues, and carefully sculptured trees and hedges, preferring a "natural" grouping of hills, dells, and babbling brooks. In keeping with the spirit of their revolutionary, populist ideas, the designers decided to create a garden for Munich's poorer inhabitants. Prince Karl Theodor had been under the impression that the Englischer Garten would be an elaborate extension of the Hofgarten, until he saw pigs and cattle grazing where his lords had once hunted for pheasant and stags, and potato patches in place of exotic flowers.

Today the pigs and potatoes are long gone, but the natural landscaping is still a joy for picnickers, lovers, and all other visitors. The **Monopteros** (love temple) atop a grassy mound south of the Chinese Tower is an attractive focal point from which to admire the splendid view of the old city.

The gardens stretch almost 5 km (3 miles) to the north, and make a lovely walk alongside the swiftly flowing River Isar. Stroll up to the Kleinhesseloher See, a boating pond, or to the little Eisbach, a branch of the Isar rushing helter-skelter under Tivoli Bridge as fast as a mountain rapid. The river encourages a particularly breakneck version of wind-surfing, a great spectator sport. However, if the mere sight of such activity exhausts you, head for the pretty Japanese Tea House (in the southwest corner), donated by Japan to commemorate the 1972 Olympic Games.

Just beyond the Tea House, on the southern edge of the garden at Prinzregentenstrasse 1, stands the **Haus der Kunst** (House of Art), a venue for temporary exhibitions.

The Haus der Kunst is another building of the Hitler era that the Allied bombardments missed. Originally known as

Free for All

During Schwabing's heyday at the turn of the 20th century, artists and writers flocked to this bohemian area of Munich. Thomas Mann lived here, as did Frank Wedekind and Bertolt Brecht, Wassily Kandinsky, and Paul Klee, as well as Franz Marc, Rainer Maria Rilke, and symbolist poet Stefan George.

A countess-turned-bohemian, Franziska zu Reventlow, chronicled the area's free love, free art, and freedom for all in her novels. Schwabing was also home to the biting satirical weekly *Simplicissimus* and to the art magazine *Jugend*, which gave its name to the German version of Art Nouveau—Jugendstil.

In 1919, the "Coffeehouse Anarchists," dramatist Ernst Toller and poet Erich Mühsam, took power after the assassination of the prime minister, Kurt Eisner. For all of six days—until the communists pushed the poets out—Schwabing ruled Bavaria, proclaiming the republic a "meadow full of flowers."

Benjamin Thompson drew inspiration for the Englisher Garten from Capability Brown and William Chambers.

the Haus der deutschen Kunst (House of German Art), it was a temple to Hitler's personal vision of a truly German art. The monotonous construction, again by Paul Ludwig Troost, was soon endowed with some popular nicknames, which included "Münchner Kunstterminus" (Munich Art Terminal) and "Palazzo Kitschi."

Another museum is to be found farther along Prinzregentenstrasse, the **Bayerisches Nationalmuseum** (the Bavarian National Museum; see page 59). From here, walk across Prinzregentenbrücke, crossing the River Isar, to the winged **Friedensengel** (or Peace Angel). High on her pillar, she surveys Prinzregententerrasse, a lovely promenade in Florentine style surrounded by gardens. Begun in 1896, the monument celebrates the 25 years of peace that followed from the German defeat of the French in 1871. Portraits of the architects of that peace—Bismarck, Kaisers Wilhelm I and II, and the generals Moltke and von der Tann—decorate the monument. The mosaics of *Peace, War, Victory,* and the *Blessings of Culture* indicate the rather ambiguous nature of the celebration.

There's nothing ambiguous, however, about the charming **Villa Stuck,** at Prinzregentenstrasse 60, which was built in 1898 for the last in Munich's line of painter-princes, Franz von Stuck. He amassed a fortune rivaling that of Lenbach by astutely combining the new artistic trends of Jugendstil symbolism with the prevailing salon taste, which demanded a certain luxury spiced with just a dash of decadence. His opulent villa is the perfect setting for the Jugendstil Museum, which is now housed here. All the interior decoration and furniture date from the turn of the century. The house is guarded by Stuck's imposing equestrian *Amazone*, and is often used as a venue for temporary exhibitions, usually of modern or contemporary art.

To the south lies the phenomenal **Deutsches Museum** (see page 62) of science and technology. On the west bank of the Isar, opposite the museum, rises the controversial European Patent Office *(Europäisches Patentamt)*. While this black steel-and-glass structure has found many admirers, others have protested against the demolition of the old neighborhood that stood in its way.

MUSEUMS

The number and diversity of museums and galleries in Munich attest to the city's importance as a cultural center. See the brief listing on page 56 for an overview of the highlights.

Alte Pinakothek

Barer Strasse 27 (Tram 27, Bus 53, U-Bahn 2). When you look at the front of this splendid building, it's easy to see

Museum and Art Gallery Highlights

(See also Munich Highlights on page 31)

Bayerisches Nationalmuseum, Prinzregentenstrasse 3, Tel. (089) 21124-1; *Tram 17; Bus 53.* German cultural history from Middle Ages to 19th century, with fine religious art. Open Tues–Sun 9:30am–5pm. DM3, children DM2. (See page 54)

BMW-Museum, Petuelring 130, Tel. (089) 38 223 307; *U-Bahn 3, Endstation Olympiazentrum; Bus 36, 136, 41, 43, 81, 184.* History of BMW against a background of world events, with classic originals. Open daily 9am to 5pm. DM5.50, children five and under free. Call Tel. (089) 38 223 306 to book factory tours. (See page 61)

Deutsches Museum, N15 Museumsinsel 1; Tel. (089) 2179-1/2179 433; *All S-Bahn lines to Isartor; Tram 18.* The largest technical and scientific museum in the world. Open daily 9am to 5pm. DM10, children DM4. (See page 62)

Glyptothek, Königsplatz 3, Tel. (089) 286 100; *U-Bahn 2, Königsplatz.* Collection of Classical Greek and Roman sculpture. Open Tues, Wed, Fri–Sun 10am–5pm, Thurs 10am–8pm. DM6, children DM3.50. Sunday free. (See page 48)

Lenbachhaus und Kuntsbau Städtische Galerie, Luisenstr. 33, Tel. (089) 233-0320 and 233-3200; *U-Bahn 2, Königsplatz.* Large collection of 19th- and 20th-century art, particularly "Blaue Reiter" school, in the Lenbachhaus. Open daily except Mon, 10am to 6pm. DM8. (See page 56)

Münchner Stadtmuseum, Sankt-Jakobs-Platz 1, Tel. (089) 23 322 370; *S-Bahn Marienplatz; U-Bahn Marienplatz or Sendlinger-Tor-Platz; Bus 52, 56.* Traces city's history and development from the middle ages. Open Tues–Sun 10am–6pm. DM5, children five and under free. (See page 56)

Museum Mensch und Natur, in Schloss Nymphenburg, Tel. (089) 176 494; *Tram 17, Bus 41.* Museum about mankind, the earth, and biological and environmental issues. Open Tues–Sun, 9am to 5pm. DM3, children under 15 free when accompanied by an adult. (See page 73)

ZAM, Westenriederstrasse 26, Tel. (089) 290 41 21; *S-Bahn Isartor; Tram 17, 18.* Center for unusual museums, including collections of chamber pots, pedal cars, and padlocks. Open daily 10am to 6pm. DM8, children DM3.

where the original brickwork ends, and the "new" brickwork —introduced when the building underwent major reconstruction in 1958 to repair the ravages of war—begins. At the back of the entry hall is a huge staircase, rising to both wings of the museum. Climbing it is certainly invigorating, but there is an elevator for those feeling less energetic.

An unusual feature of the gallery is that the layout has been organized from a chronological standpoint rather than by country and artistic movement. This enables the visitor to compare the interpretations of the different contemporary schools through the centuries.

One of the most outstanding German pieces is the *Altarpiece of the Church Fathers* (Kirchenväteraltar), painted in about 1483 by Michael Pacher. This marvelous polyptych of the saints Jerome, Augustine, Gregory, and Ambrose was acquired from the South Tyrol during the French Revolution. *The Birth of Christ* (Geburt Christi) is by Stephan Lochner of the 15th-century Cologne School.

Pieter Brueghel the Elder produced *Fool's Paradise* (Das Schlaraffenland) in 1567. The artist depicts a soldier, a peasant, and a scholar sprawled on the ground—a bitter depiction of ignorance and sloth, which Brueghel considered to be the evils of Spanish occupation.

Works by Roger van der Weyden are displayed alongside those of his contemporary Filippo Lippi, from the mid-15th century. Hans Memling's *Joys of Mary* (Freuden Mariae), and Martin Schongauer's *The Holy Family* (Heilige Familie) contrast with Botticelli's *Lamentation* (Beweinung) of 1490.

Three paintings by Giotto from the 14th century are *Last Supper* (Das letzte Abendmahl), *The Crucifixion* (die Kreuzigung) and *Christ in Purgatory* (Christus in der Vorhölle).

Albrecht Dürer's work *The Four Apostles* (Vier Apostel), from 1526, is a noble portrayal of John with Peter, and Paul with Mark. The strips of text from Martin Luther's Bible were removed by Maximilian I as he was afraid of criticism by the Jesuits. Also by Dürer is the *Self-portrait* of 1500; although imbued with great vanity (note the Christ-like pose), it is nonetheless masterful.

His contemporary, Matthias Grünewald, displays his more down-to-earth qualities in the gentle work *Conversation of St. Erasmus and St. Mauritius* (Hl. Erasmus und Hl. Mauritius im Gespräch vertieft).

The Wittelsbachs' first major acquisition was Albrecht Altdorfer's *Alexanderschlacht* (1529), which portrays Alexander's victory over Darius of Persia. This painting was a favorite of Napoleon's and hung in his apartments at St-Cloud.

An early work of Leonardo da Vinci, *Madonna with Child* (Madonna mit Kind) was probably painted in 1473, when he was 21. It already possesses much of the serene power of his mature masterpieces.

Munich is also privileged to have in its possession one of Titian's superb late pictures, the passionately dramatic *Christ Crowned with Thorns* (Dornenkrönung), finished around 1570 when the painter was almost 90. Tintoretto regarded this painting as Titian's legacy, and he bought it for his own collection. Another great work by the Venetian artist is *Madonna with Child* (Madonna mit Kind).

Raphael, whose Classical temperament so impressed Ludwig I, painted the widely admired *Madonna Tempi* in 1507. Other works from the High Renaissance are also on display here.

An amusingly coquettish picture is *Vulcan Surprises Venus and Mars* (Vulkan überrascht Venus und Mars) by Tintoretto, in which Mars is hiding under a couch, still wearing his helmet.

Anthony van Dyck's works include *Suzanna im Bade* and *Ruhe auf der Flucht*.

Peter Paul Rubens is magnificently represented by a vast panoply of his talent, including the impressive *Descent into Hell* (Höllensturz), *Lion Hunt* (Löwenjagd), and *Daughters of Leucippus* (Töchter des Leukippos). A loving portrait of Rubens' young second wife, Hélène Fourment, in her wedding dress (1630), finds the artist in a quieter mood.

Of the many self-portraits that Rembrandt painted, one of the most interesting shows the artist as a young man of 23 in 1629. From the cycle devoted to the Passion of Christ comes a particularly gripping work, *The Resurrection* (Die Auferstehung).

Typical of the work of Frans Hals is a revealing portrait of an arrogant merchant, *Willem van Heythuysen*.

Another outstanding work is the splendid Tiepolo *Adoration of the Magi* (Anbetung der Könige), which was painted in 1753 while the artist was in Bavaria. Its lavish celebration of rich reds, golds, and blues is totally appropriate to Bavaria's Baroque traditions.

If the French and Spanish Room ranks among the most popular in the museum, it may be because of Murillo's 17th-century paintings of lively young rascals. They include *Melon- and Grape-eaters* (Melonen- und Traubenesser) and *Game of Dice* (Würfelspiel).

The inspired melancholy of El Greco is evident in his *Disrobing of Christ* (Entkleidung Christi), and there's also a superb portrait of a young Spanish noble by Velázquez.

Bayerisches Nationalmuseum

Prinzregentenstrasse (Tram 17; Bus 53). The exterior of the Bavarian National Museum, built in 1900, traces in different architectural styles the artistic evolution of the periods exhibited inside—a Romanesque east wing, a later Renaissance western façade, a Baroque tower and, finally, a

Rococo west wing. The collection provides a truly magnificent span of German cultural history from the Middle Ages to the 19th century. It emphasizes both religious and secular arts and craftsmanship.

The museum holds a number of fine Romanesque and Gothic stone carvings, wooden sculptures, and paintings from churches and abbeys that have long since disappeared or been transformed. The outstanding exhibits include *Enthroned Mary* (Inthronisierte Maria) from Perugia (1200), *St. Catherine* (Hl. Katerina) from Salzburg (1420), and a beautifully ornate polychrome wood piece titled *Mary in a Rose Bower* (Maria im Rosenhag) from Straubing (1320), showing Mary as the proudest of mothers and Jesus still a playful little boy.

The highlight for many visitors is a collection of wooden sculptures by Tilman Riemenschneider, the great Late Gothic master of Germany, in the Riemenschneider-Saal. These include some powerful statues of Mary Magdalene, St. Sebastian, and the Apostles, carved in about 1500.

Another Late Gothic exhibit is one of the most frightening chiming clocks you are ever likely to come across, from the Heilbronn Monastery. The implications of *tempus fugit* were hammered home to the monks by a furious figure of Death riding a frantic-looking lion.

But you should notice, too, the admirable secular exhibits, including the Augsburger Weberstube—a room decorated with the original medieval furnishings and carvings of the Augsburg Weavers' Guild, and the Stadtmodell-Saal, which holds Jakob Sandtner's intricate 16th-century scale models of Bavarian ducal cities, Munich taking pride of place beside Ingolstadt and Landshut. Finally, look for the glorious carved doors from Egid Quirin Asam's house on Sendlinger Strasse, which depict Old and New Testament scenes.

In the museum's east wing, accessible from Lerchenfeldstrasse, is the **Prähistorische Staatssammlung** (Prehistoric Museum), which is devoted to Bavarian finds from earliest Celtic times.

BMW-Museum

Off the Petuel Ring Autobahn (U-Bahn 3, Olympiazentrum terminal; Bus 36, 136, 41, 43, 81, 184). On display at this museum that provides insight into the history of the Bavarian Motor Works are the cars, motorcycles, and aircraft engines that made BMW famous: all the classic originals are to be found here. Officials also had the excellent idea of relating a parallel history of the world events that occurred while these technical innovations in the field were being made.

The BMW-Museum stands above Munich as a modern testament to the technology of transportation.

Against a stark background, with an artful use of lighting to highlight the exhibits, contemporary history is unfolded in its political, social, and cultural dimensions. Short video films are shown and vocal testimony is heard from life-sized figures of German chancellors, American presidents, and even from celebrities such as Elvis Presley and Marilyn Monroe.

Deutsches Museum

Zweibrückenstrasse takes you to the museum (on its own little island in the Isar; S-Bahn Isartor, Tram 18). Children have all the fun here—and, since we're all children, this is a wonderful opportunity to see for yourself the largest scientific and technological collection in the world. If you were to follow the lines guiding you to each and every exhibit, you would cover nearly 20 km (12 miles).

If that all sounds too forbidding, relax in the knowledge that you don't, of course, have to see it all, and that displays have been laid out with marvelous attention to the comfort and enjoyment of visitors. The models, experimental machines, and audio-visual effects can nearly all be operated by visitors pushing buttons, turning wheels, and pulling levers. In a country that has always taken science and technology very seriously, it is reassuring to find a place where the most complex machines are, for a change, presented as monster toys for the delight and enlightenment of boys and girls.

Setting the tone of the museum is "the world's first vertical take-off jet transport plane," the Dornier Do 31 of 1967. This is no model, but the actual aircraft. Now that idea on paper may not move you very much, but the machine itself turns out to be a most endearing gizmo.

The transport section brings together almost every kind of boat, from a Native American canoe, Arab *dhow,* and Irish *curragh* (coracle) to a splendid velvet-seated gondola and a breathtaking 19th-century German sailing ship 60 m (200 ft) long. Each one of the items on display here is genuine, and not a scale model. Machinery devoted to the production of energy—including windmills, watermills, a wind-turbine of 1900 from Dresden, and an exquisite steam-powered

The Deutsches Museum offers the largest scientific and technological collection in the world.

fire engine of 1893 from Nuremberg—all assumes the beauty of sculpture.

Train enthusiasts will love the first German "Lokomobil," built in 1862 and still operating, with a gentle hiss reminiscent of a domestic steam iron. British patriots may note with interest that the Germans are pleased to have on display an exact copy of "Puffing Billy," one of the earliest English locomotives, dating from 1813. The star attraction for youngsters, however, is likely to be the model railway—complete with 204 m (670 ft) of tracks, 100-odd curves, and a vast railway station with a shunting yard of nine parallel tracks.

The cars on display range from Karl Benz's superb "Automobil Nummer 1," built in 1886, to an unpainted stainless-steel Porsche sports car from 1967, still in immaculate condition after 155,000 km (96,000 miles). These exhibits stand alongside the sublimely ridiculous *Prunkwagen* (State Coach) of Ludwig II. He had the gilded super-Rococo fairy-tale carriage designed a mere eight years before the first car. A technical note reads: *"Bremsen fehlen"*—"No brakes."

Other exhibits deal with printing, nuclear energy, musical instruments, and astronomy. There is also a first-rate planetarium described as "the most modern planetarium in the world," where you can take part in interactive astronomy and laser shows. You can even inspect the old wooden bridge built in the 12th century when Munich was no more than a small settlement (see page 12).

(See also page 73 for details of the Man and Nature museum in the Nymphenburger Palace—an excellent place to visit with children.)

☛ Glyptothek (Sculpture Museum)

Königsplatz (U-Bahn 2). Around 160 pieces, brought back from throughout the Classical world on orders of King Ludwig I, found a home in the massive, Ionic-columned edifice, rebuilt after World War II. The Glyptothek glories in its great treasure—the sculpture from the gables of the Temple of Aphaia, found on the Greek island of Aegina. These well-preserved friezes have been dated to 505 B.C. (west gable) and 485 B.C. (east gable). On them are warriors with their shields, fighting to defend the island's patron goddess, smiling that rather smug Ancient Greek smile. Look for other works of major importance: the *Apollo of Tenea,* a *Medusa,* the goddess of peace *Irene,* and the *Barberini Faun* (named after a 17th-century Italian family of classicists).

The valuable displays of the **Antikensammlungen** (Classical Art Collections) across the square from the Glypothek include a beautiful series of Greek vases and urns and, above all, the highly prized collection of Etruscan gold and silver formed by James Loeb. This German-American benefactor is known to students and scholars through the famous Loebs Classical Library of Greek and Latin texts.

Lenbachhaus und Kunstbau Städtische Galerie

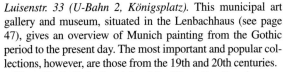

Luisenstr. 33 (U-Bahn 2, Königsplatz). This municipal art gallery and museum, situated in the Lenbachhaus (see page 47), gives an overview of Munich painting from the Gothic period to the present day. The most important and popular collections, however, are those from the 19th and 20th centuries.

The villa, built in the style of the Florentine Renaissance, was originally the residence of Franz von Lenbach. In 1929 it became a gallery for the famous Blaue Reiter collection, and it now holds the largest collection of Wassily Kandinsky paintings in Germany, in addition to canvases by Franz Marc, Gabriele Münter, Alexej von Jawlensky, August Macke, and Paul Klee. These artists were the members of Munich's pre-World War I "Blaue Reiter" (Blue Rider) school of painting. The name derives from a blue-and-black horseman drawn by Kandinsky for an almanac in 1912. Horses and the color blue were also dominant features of Franz Marc's work.

Alongside these works the Lenbachhaus collections also include a number of works by Picasso, Braque, Dalí, the German Expressionists, and a distinguished array of contemporary Americans.

The museum serves as a busy cultural center, staging concerts, lectures, and regular temporary exhibitions. There is a café on the grounds serving coffee and cold drinks, and on a hot summer day the lovely gardens and Mediterranean-style terrace are particularly inviting when you feel in need of a break from sightseeing.

Kandinsky paintings abound at Lenbachhaus, home to the Blaue Reiter school of German art.

Münchner Stadtmuseum (Municipal Museum)

St-Jakobs-Platz (S-Bahn Marienplatz; U-Bahn Marienplatz or Sendlinger-Tor-Platz; Bus 52, 56). This museum captures Munich's distinctive personality, and it's well worth spending an hour or two here to get an overview of the town's development since the Middle Ages. In the Moriskenraum is displayed the museum's main attraction: A number of jolly wooden carvings of Morris Dancers taken from the Altes Rathaus council chamber. Dated 1480, they are magnificent examples of Erasmus Grasser's Gothic style.

Maps, models, and photographs on the first floor illustrate Munich's rich history. On the second floor are 20 rooms furnished colorfully in various decorative styles from the past.

You'll see kitchens, living rooms, and bedrooms, and examples of sumptuous rooms from the Residenz, as well as cozy bourgeois homes of the 19th century, furnished with heavy Biedermeier pieces or with the more delicate Jugendstil. Highlights include a reconstruction of a very inviting 18th-century *Weinstube* (wine tavern) and an opulent artist's studio (Makart-Zimmer).

The fashion collection illustrates the evolution of styles in a town that has long been a center for German design. A poignant effort has been made to inject a light touch into the display of wartime fashions.

Children (and adults, too) will love the **Puppentheater-Sammlung** (Marionette Theater Collection) situated on the third floor, one of the largest of its kind in the world. Bavaria has for many years been a traditional center for the production of glove-puppets, shadow plays, and mechanical toys.

Neue Pinakothek

Barer Strasse 29 (Tram 27, Bus 53, U-bahn 2).

This modern museum was built in the late 1970s, replacing the original Neue Pinakothek, which was damaged beyond repair in the war. It houses an outstanding collection of paintings and sculpture from the 18th century onwards.

Characteristic of the rosy view of the 18th century that prevailed in France before the Revolution are Fragonard's Girl with Dog (Mädchen mit Hund) and Boucher's Madame de Pompadour. The romantic sunrise by Claude Lorrain (Seehafen bei Aufgang der Sonne) is a typical example of his poetic landscapes, while his Verstoßung der Hagar is an imaginative representation of Abraham's Bedouin dwelling.

Artistically, Poussin's stylized *Midas and Bacchus* and *Lamentation for Christ* (Beweinung Christi) are among the best works on display.

A selection of works by Canaletto, Guardi, Goya, and Turner give a good overview of the painting being done in the 18th and early 19th centuries. Goya is represented by the *Marquesa de Caballero*.

International art of the period around 1800 is represented by works of David, whose *Porträt der Marquise de Sorc de Thélusson* is influenced by that era's particular artistic interpretation of the French Revolution.Works by C.D. Friedrich, such as *Sudeten Mountains with Rising Mist* (Riesengebirgslandschaft mit aufsteigendem Nebel), circa 1800, are in the typical style of the early German romantics; Stieler's *Portrait of Goethe*, or Goethebildnis, from 1828, is a good example of Classicism.

Spitzweg's *The Poor Poet* (Armer Poet) is a humorous satire of the naive idealism of his contemporary artists.

Overbeck's *Italia und Germania* (1811–1828) is a striking example of the German Nazarene school, also known as the Lucas Brotherhood.

Admirers of Cézanne, Gauguin, Manet, Monet, and Van Gogh can spend many a happy hour here. Van Gogh's Sunflowers (1888) is a particularly popular work that always draws admirers.

As you move on to the late 19th and early 20th century exhibits, notice the contrast between the social realism of Max Liebermann and the symbolism of the Jugendstil, represented by Gustav Klimt and Max Klinger.

Until the brand new Pinakothek der Moderne opens nearby in 2002, both the Neue and Alte Pinatotheks are also home to works by Kandinsky, Mondrian, Kokoschka, Chagall, and other artists formerly represented in the now closed State Gallery for Modern Art. While these more recent works are quite comfortable in the Neue Pinakothek, they don't always sit quite so well in the Alte Pinakothek, though they do make a fascinating contrast to the centuries-old paintings alongside them.

Residenzmuseum

The museum's main entrance is on Max-Joseph-Platz (S-Bahn Marienplatz; U-Bahn 3, 4, 5, 6 Odeonsplatz; Tram 19; Bus 53). The Residenz is so huge—112 rooms, halls, and galleries, in addition to the 10 rooms of the Schatzkammer (Treasure Chamber)—that, for guided tours, the museum is divided up into two itineraries, one offered in the morning, the other in the afternoon. Both tours include some of the more important rooms and provide a good overall impression of the Wittelsbach era, so one tour is sufficient. You can, alternatively, wander through the rooms on your own without a guide.

Below are some of the rooms you can visit.

Degenerates Forever!

Hitler's speech inaugurating the Haus der Deutschen Kunst in 1937 attacked the "obscenities" of avant-garde art and forbade any painter to use colors that the "normal" eye could not perceive in nature. Two exhibitions were held to distinguish so-called great German art from that designated "degenerate art."

The trouble was that the "degenerate" show was far more popular, and attracted 2 million visitors, five times as many as the other exhibition. Afterwards, many of these paintings, including works by Kandinsky, Mondrian, Kokoschka, and Chagall, were hidden away or sold abroad for valuable foreign currency. Today they are displayed in the Alte and Neue Pinakothek, and will take up residence in their new home, the Pinakothek Der Moderne, in 2002.

Ahnengalerie (Gallery of the Ancestors). Here you can acquaint yourself with a mere 121 of the Wittelsbachs, starting with Duke Theodor, who lived around the year 700.

Antiquarium. This monumental 70-m- (225-ft-) long Renaissance library was designed by Friedrich Sustris for Duke Albrecht V in 1558. The room takes its name from the 16th-century busts of ancient Greek and Roman leaders on display.

Porcelain collections. This prodigious array of French, English, and German porcelain includes the delicate work of Meissen, from near Dresden, as well as local pieces produced in Nymphenburg. Japanese and Chinese porcelain and superb lacquer work form part of a separate exhibit.

Grottenhof. Designed by Sustris in 1581, this is perhaps the most elegant courtyard in the Residenz, distinguished by the graceful arcade along the eastern side and by Hubert Ger-

Visit the Treasure Chamber of the Residenzmuseum and see the crown jewels, among other Wittelsbach heirlooms.

hard's fine bronze Perseus fountain set in the middle. The Grottenwand, or Grotto Wall (with a fountain in an alcove), gives the courtyard its name. A statue of Mercury is flanked by Nubian slaves, fish-tailed satyrs, nymphs, and parrots, and the ensemble is encrusted with many thousands of mussel, scallop, and winkle shells.

Reiche Zimmer. Together these State Rooms provide the most outstanding example of Rococo décor in Germany. Cuvilliés designed them in 1729, and his jewel among jewels was the Grüne Galerie (Green Gallery), in which you will want to linger. The Spiegelkabinett (Cabinet of Mirrors), Miniaturenkabinett, and Chinesisches Kabinett are equally fascinating.

Hofkapelle and Reiche Kapelle. Of these charmingly intimate chapels, the first was originally set aside for common courtiers, while the second was for the exclusive use of the Wittelsbachs.

Schatzkammer (Treasure Chamber). A separate tour is dedicated to viewing the dynasty's spectacular collection of jewelry, gold, silver, crystal, and enamelware, amassed over the course of 1,000 years. One of the earliest of the Wittelsbach heirlooms is a communion goblet dating from about 890, known as the Arnulfziborium (Arnolph's Ciborium).

ROYAL RETREATS

Schloss Nymphenburg, now inside the ever-expanding city limits, was the Wittelsbachs' summer refuge, away from the heat of the Residenz in the city center. This gleaming palace is set in extensive grounds with fountains, ponds, and four enchanting garden pavilions—it's the perfect place to stroll and recall the *dolce far niente* of the Wittelsbach days, when they played at nymphs and shepherds here and forgot all about the worries of state. There's no U-Bahn station at the palace, but if you don't have a car for the 8-km (5-mile) ride, a No. 17 tram or No. 41 bus will take you there. The palace and museums are closed on Monday.

In 1662 Princess Henriette Adelaide presented to her husband his new son and heir. The birth of the child inspired the architects of the time to build both the Theatinerkirche and the Nymphenburg. The palace had modest enough beginnings as a small summer villa, but it grew over the next century as each succeeding ruler added another wing or his own little pavilion and changed the landscaping of the gardens. Max Emmanuel, the little baby who was the cause of it all, grew up with the ambition of emulating Louis XIV's Versailles. While he may not have succeeded completely in this, the French armies appreciated his efforts and made Nymphenburg their headquarters in 1800.

The palace is approached by a long canal with avenues on either bank leading to a semicircle of lawns, the Schlossrondell, which is the site of the building containing the royal porcelain factory (see Shopping, page 86). In the central edifice of the palace proper are galleries of fine 18th-century stucco work and ceiling frescoes. The majestic two-story ban-

Take the time to stroll the expansive grounds of the Schloss Nymphenburg.

quet hall, **Steiner Saal** (Stone Hall), contains several lively frescoes by Johann Baptist Zimmermann on the theme *Nymphen huldigen der Göttin Flora* (Nymphs Pay Homage to the Goddess Flora).

To the south, the first pavilion is the home of the famous **Schönheitengalerie** (Gallery of Beautiful Women). Ludwig I commissioned Joseph Stieler to paint these portraits of Munich's most beautiful young women. The lady with the belt of snakes and whip in hand, the notorious Lola Montez, was likely his mistress. She was born Mary Dolores Eliza Rosanna Gilbert, daughter of an Irish adventurer. As her mother was reputedly a Spanish countess, she went on stage as Señora Maria de los Dolores Porris y Móntez (see page 21).

The **Marstallmuseum,** a dazzling collection of state coaches used for coronations, weddings, and other royal frolics, has been installed in the south wing, in what was once the royal stables. Starting from the extravagance of Karl Albrecht's 18th-century coronation coaches, the vehicles went on to achieve a state of ornamental delirium under Ludwig II. Look for his Nymphenschlitten (Nymph sleigh), designed for escapades in the Alps. On the first floor is the beautiful **Bäuml** collection of Nymphenburg porcelain, covering examples of the entire output from the Nymphenburg factory, from the early days in the 18th century to the 1920s. The Castle Lustheim also has a fine porcelain collection.

Also in the Nymphenburg palace is the extensive **Museum Mensch und Natur** (Man and Nature Museum), where the exhibits successfully bring this subject to life and hold the attention of children (and adults) of all ages through the use of films, audio-visual programs, and interactive models. The museum covers a variety of topics, including an exploration of the history of the planet and of life on earth, emphasizing the variety of forms of life and the importance of their interaction. The position of man in the universe and his responsibilities towards the environment are important themes, and numerous ecological topics are explored, such as land erosion, population growth, and hunger.

The palace **gardens** were originally laid out in a subdued Italian style for Henriette Adelaide, but her son's taste was for the more grandiose French manner. Later, Ludwig von Sckell, landscape artist of the Englischer Garten, was brought in, and the park lost some of its formality, which makes for a more relaxed stroll. However, the restyling left the Baroque and Rococo pavilions a little isolated, somewhat like long-standing tenants who stayed on in a house while new owners changed all the furniture around them. Traces of the former Classical geometry can be seen in the symmetry of the Schlossrondell and the rectangular Grosse Parterre directly to the west of the central edifice. The palace grounds are decorated here and there with some attractive marble statues of Greek gods by Dominikus Auliczek and others.

Off to the left lies **Amalienburg,** one of the prettiest little hunting lodges in the country. Construction began in 1734 by the same three men who worked on the opulent State Rooms of the Residenz—architect François de Cuvilliés, sculptor Joachim Dietrich, and stucco artist Johann Baptist Zimmermann. Wander round the rooms where the hunting dogs and rifles were kept, the Pheasant Room next to the blue-and-white, Dutch-tiled kitchen and, above all, enjoy the brilliant silver-and-pastel-yellow Rococo **Spiegelsaal** (Hall of Mirrors). This was originally the pavilion's entrance.

Continue west to find the **Badenburg** (Bath Pavilion), fitted with Delft china fixtures that are an interior decorator's dream, and the Grosser See, a large pond dotted with islands. Overlooking it is a promontory topped by a love temple modeled after Rome's Temple of Vesta, goddess of fire.

North of the central canal, with its spectacular cascade of water, is another, smaller pond. On the far side of it stands the Pagodenburg, an octagonal tea pavilion with several exotic black-and-red-lacquered Chinese chambers upstairs.

The fourth of the park's pavilions is the **Magdalenenklause** (Hermitage), built for the private meditations of Max Emmanuel in 1725. The dominant theme of the paintings and sculptures inside is penitence. Don't be surprised that the building is a crumbling ruin; the cracks and flaking plaster were deliberately incorporated into the mock Romanesque and Gothic structure, and a Moorish minaret was thrown in too.

The area lying north of the park has been given over to the **Neuer Botanischer Garten** (New Botanical Gardens), entered from Menzinger Strasse. The Arboretum at the west end of the gardens has been cleverly landscaped to resemble different climatic regions of the world, complete with their appropriate flora—pine forest, Arctic tundra, heath and moorland, desert dunes, the steppes, and Alpine country are here—alongside an artificial pond.

After the flamboyance of Nymphenburg, go farther west (by car or number 73 bus from the end of Menzinger Strasse) to the refreshing simplicity of **Schloss Blutenburg,** now a convent. It's worth visiting for the palace chapel, of a superb Late Gothic type rare in this part of Bavaria. The three altars display splendid paintings by Jan Polack, done in 1491: the *Holy Trinity* (high altar), *Christ Enthroned* (on the left), and the *Annunciation* (to the right). On the walls are hung some beautiful polychrome wooden sculptures of the Apostles, Mary, and a resurrected Christ. These figures date from around 1500.

Finish your tour in nearby Pippinger Strasse and go into **Pfarrkirche St. Wolfgang** (St. Wolfgang's Parish Church). A number of frescoes attributed to Polack (1479) decorate the admirably serene interior, and there are also three delicately carved wooden altars from the same period. The quiet of the church is the perfect spot for meditation at the end of a long day.

EXCURSIONS

To take the full measure of Munich, you must visit its hinterland, the beautiful Bavarian countryside. This is the land of picturesque lakes, little country churches, and Ludwig II's crazy castles. Visitors without a car can book a place on one of the many tours that are organized by the Munich-Upper Bavaria Tourist Office (see page 124). Each tour we propose can be done easily in one day.

Ludwig's Follies

The two Ludwig II castles situated to the south of Munich, Neuschwanstein and Linderhof, are best visited separately. Choose one, or, if that's not enough for you, then add the other to your itinerary.

Follow the A96 and B12 to **Landsberg am Lech** (with its interesting medieval town center), and then take the B17, the Deutsche Alpenstrasse (German Alpine Road). Stop off at Steingaden to visit the lovely **St. Johann Baptist Church,** which retains much of its 12th-century Romanesque exterior. You'll also enjoy the pleasant walk in the old cloister.

It's worth making a detour to the east to visit the magnificent **Wieskirche,** a pilgrimage church of 1754 designed by

Dominikus Zimmermann. The church's ceiling is decorated with a sublime fresco by his brother Johann Baptist, which depicts Christ dispensing divine mercy. In its architecture and decoration, the church is a consummate work—perfect to the last Rococo detail.

Return to the main road for the journey to the more pagan **Neuschwanstein** (follow the signs to the castle or look for signs to "Füssen"). A visit in 1867 to the medieval castle of Wartburg, Thuringia, first fired Ludwig's imagination with a vision of the Minnesänger, the minstrels of the 12th century, and he decided to build a castle that would recapture the aura of that romantic era.

Ludwig replaced a ruined mountain retreat of his father's in the Schwangau with an extraordinary white-turreted castle. Set in the midst of a forest of firs and pines, it overlooks the gorge of Pöllat and Lake Forggen. Be sure to visit the great dreamer's throne room, and try to imagine, as did Ludwig, the minstrel contests of another age in the Sängersaal. Wagnerians will recognize the sculptural and painted allusions to *Tannhäuser*, *Die Meistersinger von Nürnberg,* and *Tristan und Isolde*.

While the Neuschwanstein castle was being built, Ludwig kept an eye on its progress from the neighbor-

The Schloss Linderhof is just one of many extravagances built by Ludwig I.

The Pilatushaus stands out as one of the finest 18th-century façades in Oberammergau.

ing castle of **Hohenschwangau,** just 1 km (half a mile) away. This Neo-Gothic building had been constructed by his father, Maximilian II. In fact, Neuschwanstein and Hohenschwangau collectively are known as "die Königsschlösser." Take a look at the music room, with its display of Wagner memorabilia (the composer stayed at Hohenschwangau) and Ludwig's bedroom, noted for its star-studded ceiling and the intricately carved bed.

To reach the second of Ludwig's dream castles, take the Garmisch-Partenkirchen Autobahn from Munich, turning off west to **Ettal.** Set in a gently curving valley is a lovely Benedictine monastery with a fine domed church. Stop and admire Johann Jakob Zeiller's 18th-century fresco of the life of St. Benedict. Then go on to **Oberammergau,** setting for the famous ten-yearly Passion Play, inaugurated in the plague year of 1633. In the town are preserved some very attractive 18th-century façades, painted on the houses by the so-called *Lüftlmaler* (air painter), Franz Zwinck. The best ones are on Pilatushaus and Geroldhaus.

Ludwig's favorite castle, **Linderhof,** was the embodiment of his Baroque fantasies. The palace, inspired by the Grand Trianon of Versailles, is opulent inside and out. Quite apart from the carefully tailored landscape of pond and park, you could be excused for thinking that the whole romantic Alpine backdrop of the fabulous Graswangtal had been created from Ludwig's imagination. Only the Venus Grotto, carved out of the mountainside and forming another Wagnerian motif from *Tannhäuser*, is in fact man-made.

The Lakes

Ammersee (35 km southwest of Munich on the A96) is a delightful place for long walks along the lake or up into the wooded hills. Make for the Benedictine Abbey of **Andechs** in the hills that overlook Ammersee from the east. The church was put up in the 15th century and was redecorated in the Rococo style by Johann Baptist Zimmermann. The monastery brewery produces first-rate beer.

For **Starnberger See,** the best route is along the S-Bahn or the Garmisch-Partenkirchen Autobahn southwest. Relax in the area's quiet, rural scenery and wander along the peaceful rush-fringed shoreline. It was here that Ludwig II drowned in 1886 (see page 22) after being held at Schloss Berg, near the resort town of Starnberg.

Tegernsee (Salzburg Autobahn, Holzkirchen exit) was once a focal point of German culture, dating back to the eighth century. Its monastery held a library that, in 1500, was bigger than the one in the Vatican. The French Revolution meant secularization and the removal of the monastery's treasures to Munich. Today the Benedictine Abbey houses a beer hall, and Tegernsee ranks as a high center of German social life. Join the élite of Munich society as they congregate around the lake, partake of the iodized waters at Bad Wiessee, and dine out in Rottach.

Chiemsee (to the southeast of Munich on the Salzburg Autobahn) is the largest lake in Bavaria and the backdrop for

Ludwig II's most ambitious castle. **Herrenchiemsee** is situated on an island, the Herreninsel, at the western end of the lake (you can take a boat out from the jetty at Stock). Ludwig started work on it in 1878, but ran out of money, and time, in 1886. Nevertheless, he made a valiant attempt at recreating the grandeur of Versailles, and the magnificent Spiegelsaal (Hall of Mirrors) can certainly bear comparison with the Galerie des Glaces. It is a homage to the king Ludwig admired most, Louis XIV.

On another island nearby is **Frauenchiemsee** (St. Mary's Monastery Church), together with some charming little fishing cottages. The church's fine 13th-century frescoes only recently came to light. Chiemsee is probably the most romantic of Bavaria's resort lakes.

North of Munich

This excursion takes in some of the lightest and most somber aspects of Bavaria's past. You'll probably want to start at the darker end and relax afterwards in the lighter.

Dachau (17 km/11 miles northwest on B304, or take the S-Bahn, Line 2) used to be known as a pretty, sleepy little village that was a favorite with painters. Visitors came for the remains of a 16th-century château and the fine 18th-century façades on many of its houses. Then, on 20 March 1933, after Hitler had been in power for a mere 48 days, Dachau was designated as the site of the first Nazi concentration camp. It was established in a disused gunpowder factory. Today, while you can still appreciate the charming town center, you should also visit the **Concentration Camp Museum.** Follow the signs (just like one you'll see in a 1930s photo on display in the museum), to the "Konzentrationslager." There are also signs reading "KZ-Concentration Camp Museum." You can take a bus or taxi from the S-Bahn station, but you should check on the times of buses going back to the station.

The museum was built on the site of the camp by the International Dachau Committee, funded by the Bavarian state government. Discreetly, but uncompromisingly, without unnecessary pathos, exhibitions document the camp's sinister history. You'll see photos, uniforms worn by guards and officers, and the insignia that were used to distinguish the prisoners—black for political dissidents, pink for homosexuals, yellow for Jews. Dachau was not one of the leading centers for extermination—even so, 31,951 deaths were recorded between 1933 and 1945—but served as a detention camp for major political prisoners and as a research station for the experiments that were carried out in Auschwitz. About 100,000 inmates were interned here. In addition to the comprehensive museum, you can see the original crematorium and gas chambers (labeled "Bad" for showers), built but never used, as well as reconstructed prison barracks. Chapels and a synagogue are provided for visitors' prayers.

Continue east to **Schloss Schleissheim** and re-enter the Baroque world of Max Emmanuel. The Neues Schloss has a glorious staircase with frescoes by Cosmas Damian Asam. Beautiful stucco work adorns banqueting halls and galleries such as the Barockgalerie, containing a fine collection of 17th-century Dutch and Flemish paintings.

The **gardens** are the triumph here, a victory for the French style of landscaping, with waterfall, canals, and flowerbeds by Carbonet and Dominique Girard, a disciple of the French master André Le Nôtre. At the eastern end, just under a mile away, is **Schloss Lustheim,** a hunting lodge. After admiring its collection of Meissen porcelain, take time out for tea.

WHAT TO DO

ENTERTAINMENT

Munich has no problem in providing entertainment—there's something here to suit every taste. First and foremost, Munich is a city of music, with four major symphony orchestras: the Bavarian State Orchestra, Munich Philharmonic, Bavarian Radio Symphony, and Graunke Symphony Orchestra. The main concerts are performed at the Gasteig Kulturzentrum, an enormous complex that incorporates several concert halls under one roof.

In summer there are open-air concerts in the Hofgarten, brass bands strike up at the Chinese Tower in the Englischer Garten, or you can enjoy concerts in the palatial setting of Blutenburg, Nymphenburg, Schloss Dachau, or the Grosser Saal at Schleissheim. Music does not stop during the winter, when church concerts are performed in the Frauenkirche, and churches of St. Michael and St. Peter.

Opera has been an attraction in Munich for centuries. The town vies with Bayreuth for performances of Wagner, and the works of Mozart and Richard Strauss are favorites. Though the Italians take second place, Verdi, Rossini, and Donizetti are by no means neglected. The majestic Nationaltheater makes every opera evening seem like a gala. The Bavarian State Orchestra plays under the world's greatest conductors, and the summer festival (*Münchner Festspiele*) in July and August attracts the very best international singers to the city. A Munich Season (*Münchner Saison*) from December to February offers the special joy of Mozart operas in the Cuvilliéstheater. In summer, open-air opera is staged in the pleasant Brunnenhof courtyard of the gigantic Residenz.

Inside the concert hall Cuvilliéstheater, just one of the cultural venues located within the Residenz.

Jazz is a favorite in Munich; American and European musicians play nightly in many places, especially Schwabing. You can also find jazz musicians in the Biergarten during the summer. A big summer festival is staged at Olympic Hall.

If your German is up to it, try the first-rate **theater.** Classical and contemporary plays are performed at the Residenz-theater (Max-Joseph-Platz 1) and the Deutsches Theater (Schwanthalerstrasse 13). The smaller theaters of Schwabing provide a more avant-garde repertoire, as does the open-air theater at Olympiapark.

For those interested in political cabaret, Schwabing is still the best place to go. Most troupes have the longevity of a butterfly; the best-established one is the Münchner Lach- und Schiessgesellschaft (on the corner of Haimhauser/Ursulastrasse).

Nightclubs are found in the center of town and Schwabing, but beer halls are likely to provide the most relaxed evening entertainment.

If you feel like a change from cultural activity, try the delightful **Hellabrunn Zoo** (U3 underground to Thalkirchen from Marienplatz). Here, animals are grouped according to their continent of origin, and you'll see zoological curiosities such as the tarpan, a kind of horse, and the white-tailed gnu. The antics of the chimps "working out" in their own private gym attract appreciative audiences.

FESTIVALS

The people of Munich always seem to have something to celebrate. More than one hundred days a year are officially given over to festivals, processions, banquets, and street dances commemorating events such as the arrival of the first strong beer of the year (*Starkbierzeit*) or the departure—several centuries ago!—of this plague or that occupying army. In fact, any excuse will do.

Fasching (carnival) is almost as mad in Munich as it is in the Rhineland. It runs from 7 January. Some 2,500 balls are held all over town for policemen and doctors, lawyers and butchers, artists and plumbers. There are masked processions, and market women at the Viktualienmarkt have their fling at midday on Shrove Tuesday.

The biggest blow-out of all is the **Oktoberfest**. This began when the Crown Prince, Ludwig (later Ludwig I), celebrated his marriage to Princess Theresa in October 1810 with a horse race, to which everybody came. They came again the next year, too, and the year after, and they're still coming from all over the world. Although the horse race has been dropped and the festivities now take place during the warmer second half of September, the blushing bride is not forgotten—the name of the site on which the Oktoberfest is held is Theresienwiese, west of the Innenstadt. Locals, however, refer to it as the "Wies'n," which is also a nickname for the festival. During the two weeks of Oktoberfest, revelers consume gargantuan quan-

Calendar of Events

For the most up-to-date information on the city's festivals and arts calendar, including a current list of times and dates, ask the tourist information office for their monthly program of events, or consult the local press.

Fasching. Starts 7 January. Costumed balls and processions.

Starkbierzeit. Week including 19 March. Making and sampling of special strong beers, always ending in "-ator."

Frühlingsfest (Spring Fair). End of April. Fun fair, concerts.

Auer Dult Huge flea market held for eight days from the last Sat in April. Also held in July and October.

Stadtgründungsfest (Foundation of the City). Weekend around the 14th of June. Fun fair.

Corpus Christi (June). Colorful street processions. People and horses wear traditional costumes.

Nymphenburger Schloßkonzerte. June/July. Open-air concerts in the grounds of Nymphenburg.

Opernfestspiele. 3 weeks in July. A variety of opera performances that take place at Nationaltheater, Cuvilliéstheater, and elsewhere.

Oktoberfest. 16 days up to the first Sunday in October. Commemorates the marriage of Ludwig I to Princess Theresa in 1810. Beer drinking, fun fair, processions.

Six-Day-Cycle Race (November). Two-wheeled marathon at the Olympiahalle. Entertainment, beer, and food.

Christkindlmarkt (Christchild market). December. Market offering crafts and gifts for the season on Marienplatz and also around Frauenkirche.

tities of beer, toted around ten litres at a time by the hefty beermaids. This brew washes down hundreds of thousands of barbecued chickens and thousands of sausages, and the operator of a monster roasting spit boasts that he turns out up to 60 whole oxen during the festival. And to work all that off, there's the fun of the fair, with roller-coasters, giant ferris-wheel, and dodgem cars. To scare it off, visit Schichtl's age-old horror show.

Signs: *Eingang* – entrance/*Ausgang, Ausfahrt* – exit

SHOPPING

Munich is an elegant town, the capital of Germany's fashion industry, so there's no lack of chic boutiques, especially on Theatinerstrasse, Maximilianstrasse, and on Schwabing's Leopoldstrasse. Munich is also the place for the world's best selection of well-tailored garments (coats, jackets, and suits) made in Loden cloth, a Bavarian specialty. This waterproof wool fabric, originally developed for hunters, has kept the people of Munich warm for over a hundred years.

You may even care to try the Bavarian costume (*Tracht*). There are smart green-collared gray jackets for men or, for women, gaily colored dirndl dresses with a full gathered skirt and fitted bodice.

German leather goods and sportswear are good buys, and Lederhosen, those slap-happy traditional shorts for Bavarians, may amuse the children.

Nymphenburg porcelain is still turned out in traditional Rococo designs. You can view pieces (and make a purchase) at the Nymphenburger Schlossrondell's factory. Connoisseurs should be on the look-out for old Meissen or modern Rosenthal.

German-manufactured cutlery, kitchen utensils, and electronic gadgets are of a very high standard and superbly designed. You might also like to consider linens, in modern or traditional designs, which are renowned for their good old-fashioned quality. A great way to save on winter heating bills is to get a sumptuous duck- or goose-down *Federbett* or eiderdown, another good buy.

German binoculars and telescopes are widely appreciated and, although the competition from Japan is keen, there are still many excellent cameras on the market, especially at the miniature end of the range.

Shopping for high-quality German goods is made easy in modern Munich.

Germany has always produced excellent children's toys; its industrial prowess is reflected in the intricate building sets and model trains.

The presence of so many great orchestras and musicians in Germany means that the selection of records here is probably second only to the United States. The production of musical instruments, such as the finest grand pianos, violins, and even harmonicas, also enjoys a venerable reputation.

In addition to searching for bargains in the exclusive shops in the city center, keep your eyes open for flea markets. They pop up all over Schwabing whenever students and artists fall behind on the rent money, but the best are the seasonal ones known as "Auer Dult," dating back to the 14th century. These take place over eight days, three times a year (May, July, and October) in the Au district (around Mariahilfplatz south of the

You don't have to be a world-class athlete to enjoy the facilities at Olympiapark.

Deutsches Museum). It is clear that these markets turn up some interesting bargains from the number of city-center antiques dealers on the spot early in the morning. Just beat them to it.

SPORTS

The city's great boon to sports lovers was the construction of the Olympic facilities in 1972. Visitors and regulars alike can participate in the daily program of events and training held at the Gesundheitspark (Health Park) of the Olympic Stadium. Contact the Municipal Sports Office (Städtisches Sportamt, Tel. (089) 30 672 414) for information.

The swimming pool at the Olympia Schwimmhalle can be used by anyone, as can eight other indoor and ten open-air pools dotted around the town. The latter all provide lawns for sunbathing. All year round, ice-skating fans congregate at the Olympic ice rink and speed-skating track.

Munich has its share of tennis courts, too: the best are at Olympiapark northeast of the Innenstadt, and in the Englischer Garten, but the most attractive are on the lavish grounds of Schloss Nymphenburg.

While serious runners might want to hit the track in the Olympic Stadium, jogging and running in the Englischer

Garten is more fun, especially the stretch along the River Isar. Running in the city is also very pleasant, as long as you get out early enough (before 7am) to avoid the traffic. For some good exercise and lovely scenery, try cycling the 14 km (9 miles) along the river path to Ismaning, or any of the bike routes throughout Munich.

Mileage of cars is calculated in liters per 100 km.

There are 15 golf courses located within a circle of 20 km (12 miles) around the city. On the southwest edge of town, Strasslach has excellent courses. Courses in the Munich area include Feldafing, Olching, Worthsee, and Margarethenhof am Tegernsee. Note that many golf courses are closed on Mondays.

For people who don't want to exert themselves, delightful raft trips (*Flossfahrten*) are organized on the weekends. You can drift slowly down the Isar from Wolfratshausen to Munich, while the beer flows and brass bands play.

Spectator sports are dominated by soccer; one of the most successful teams in Europe, Bayern München (Bayer Munich), plays at the Olympic Stadium. Rowing and canoeing events are held at Schloss Schleissheim. To the east of the city center, horseracing is held at Riem and trotting takes place at Daglfing.

Farther out of Munich, you can do some serious sailing or windsurfing on the Ammersee, and on Starnberger See and Tegernsee. The local lakes and rivers also offer good fishing.

If you want to take part in deer and wild boar hunting in the Bavarian forests, apply to the German Hunting Association for a license (Deutscher Jagdschutzverband, J Henry Strasse 26, Bonn).

Hiking is a major pastime, especially as you approach the Bavarian Alps. Just 97 km (61 miles) from Munich, Garmisch-Partenkirchen provides guides for mountain climbing. There are plenty of peaks to tackle, including the 2,963-m- (9,721-ft-) high Zugspitze.

Once you are in the Alps, the whole range of winter sports is at your disposal. Garmisch has, in addition to its skiing (and a very professional ski school), its own Olympic rink for skating and ice hockey. The more sedate can try curling, and for the more adventurous there is a bobsled run.

CHILDREN

Munich, complete with fairy-tale buildings, parks, and gardens, is a wonderful city for children, at any time of year and in any weather. Many of the museums listed on pages 57 to 71 are suitable for children; the **Deutsches Museum** is of particular interest (see page 62), with plenty of fascinating machines and models to play with, and hands-on exhibits for children to operate for themselves. The **Museum Mensch und Natur** (see page 56) is an excellent museum that explores a variety of issues on the subject of man, nature and ecology, and is full of weird and wonderful exhibits sure to keep youngsters of all ages entertained. You could also try the **Marionette Collection** in the Stadtmuseum (see page 66); the **Deutsches Jagd- und Fischereimuseum** (the hunting and fishing museum, see also page 34), with exhibits on wild animals, hunting techniques, weapons and trophies, and the story of fishing equipment through the ages; and the **Spielzeugmuseum** (toy museum, in the old town hall) showing examples from 200 years of toys. The **ZAM** (center for unusual museums, see page 56) has an Easter Bunny Museum and also gives children the chance to drive their own car. The new Siemens Forum on Oskar-Von-Miller-Ring presents 140 years of electronics history in a fun, hands-on way.

The Spielzeugmuseum (toy museum) is bound to offer something of interest to your children.

If the weather is too good to stay indoors, try a visit to the Munich Zoo (Tierpark Hellabrunn). Picnicking in the Englischer Garten or taking a bike ride down the beautiful paths along the Isar River is sure to delight, or you can join the crowds cooling off in the Isar from the Prater Insel, near the Maximilian Bridge.

Two wonderful theaters for children exist in Munich: the Puppentheater (Glove-puppet Theater) in the Künstlerhaus on Lenbachplatz, and the Marionettentheater, Blumenstrasse 29a, near Sendlinger Tor. Both put on performances for children in the afternoon as well as staging marionette opera for adults in the evening.

EATING OUT

Eating and drinking in Bavaria in general, and in Munich in particular, are favorite leisure pursuits. Conviviality reigns supreme, both in the high temples of gastronomy and at the long, communal tables of the *Bräuhaus* and *Gaststätte*.

Where to Eat

With its great prosperity and tradition of good living, Munich has more refined restaurants than might be expected by those who think of German cuisine as being merely heavy and unimaginative. Most of them are in Maximilianstrasse, Residenzstrasse, and Theatinerstrasse, along Schwabing's Leopoldstrasse, and in Prinzregentenstrasse at the southern end of the Englischer Garten. In some of the better establishments you will also find high-quality delicatessens.

Munich's growing sophistication is such nowadays that elegance, however casual, is considered to be more important than the traditional formality of ties for men or skirts for women. It's a good idea to reserve a table in advance at the smarter places. Although a service charge of 15 percent is already included in the bill, not many people have been known to refuse a little extra.

The niceties of dress and advance reservations are not a problem at the more popular *Gaststätte* or *Bräuhaus*—literally meaning "brewery," but in actual fact a beer hall. These establishments usually serve full meals in addition to beer, though in the bigger halls you should make sure you sit in the dining section. All the great breweries have their own beer halls in Munich, and beer gardens, too, many of them with brass bands. In the inner city, the beer halls also provide an openair *Bierkeller*. The popular beer gardens of the Englischer Garten are at the Chinese Tower, at the Hirschau, and beside the Kleinhesseloher See. *Weinstuben* (taverns), less numerous in the beer country of Bavaria than in other regions of Germany, serve wine by the glass rather than by the carafe or bottle, and provide meals.

In a separate category is the *Konditorei* (a café-cum-pastry shop), the bourgeois fairy-land where you can spend a whole afternoon reading the newspapers provided. This is the perfect place for a feast of pastry, ice cream, coffee, tea, and fruit juices, with even a good selection of wines. Most provide a limited selection of egg dishes, light snacks, and salads.

Munich also has its quota of fast-food chains and myriad ethnic restaurants; the Italian, Greek, and Balkan ones are particularly worth trying.

Meal Times

Lunch (*Mittagessen*) is usually served from 11:30 am to 2 pm, dinner (*Abendessen*) from 6:30 pm to 8:30 pm (10:30 pm or 11 pm in large establishments). The majority of Germans like to eat their main meal in the middle of the day, and generally prefer a lighter supper (*Abendbrot*, or "evening

Local Customs

In a *Gaststätte* or *Bräuhaus,* you'll sometimes come across a sign on one of the long tables proclaiming *"Stammtisch."* This means the seats have been reserved for regulars—club, firm, or big family. Otherwise strangers usually sit together, after a polite query as to whether one of the empty places is *"frei."* Fellow diners usually wish each other *"Mahlzeit"* or *"Guten Appetit."*

It may come as a surprise that each bread roll *(Semmel)* and pretzel is charged separately; you're expected to keep a count of how many you've eaten.

bread") at night, of cold meats and cheeses, possibly eaten with a salad.

Breakfast (Frühstück)

Germans start the day with a meal that is a bit more substantial than the typical "Continental" breakfast. The distinctive touch is the selection of cold meats—including ham, salami, and liver sausage (*leberwurst*)—and cheese served with the bread. You will not find just one kind of bread, but a wide variety—brown (rye with caraway seeds), as well as rich black (*pumpernickel*) and white. If you like boiled eggs, try *eier im glas*—two four-minute eggs served whole, already shelled, in a glass dish. And with it all comes tea, hot chocolate, or coffee—stronger than the Anglo-American variety, but weaker than its French or Italian counterpart.

Soups and Starters

Bavarians specialize in excellent *Leberknödlsuppe*, a soup made with spicy dumplings of flour, bread crumbs, beef liver, onions, marjoram, and garlic. *Kartoffelsuppe* contains potatoes, celery, leek, and parsnip. Other popular soups are made with beans (*Bohnen-*

All manner of meats can be had in Munich. The meat counter at Dallmayr is testament to the abundance.

suppe) or lentils (*Linsensuppe*), with pieces of sausage added to the mix.

If you prefer an hors d'oeuvre, try smoked calf's tongue served with a little horseradish sauce (*Kalbszüngerl*) or pork tongue boiled with a seasoning of juniper berries, bay leaves, and peppercorns, accompanied by sauerkraut (*Schweinszüngerl im Kraut*).

Bavarian Specialities

The pig and the calf dominate Bavarian main dishes, often in combination. Pork or veal can be either pot-roasted (*Kalbs-* or *Schweinebraten*) or grilled on a spit (*am Spieß*) to obtain a marvelous crackling skin. The Munich speciality is spit-roast *Schweinehaxen*, hock of pork, sold in halves or whole. Be careful when ordering; a half is a meal unto itself. The ultimate delicious roast is *Spanferkel*, or suckling pig. For a change, sample the excellent game when in season—venison, hare, partridge, and pheasant.

Keeping It Flowing

Most of the time, there are enough big festivals to keep the beer flowing, but Munich brewers can't bear slack periods.

In the third and fourth weeks before Easter, the so-called Starkbierzeit (Strong-beer Time), beer festivals promote their Märzenbier (March Ale). After Easter comes the Maibockzeit, when they push the strong dark stuff. In the summer, everybody's thirsty enough not to need too much prompting.

Then comes the Oktoberfest (see page 84), the ultimate in beer festivals, when every brewery participates in a colorful parade of horse-drawn wagons. Christmas and Fasching (carnival) tide the brewers over till it's time again for Märzenbier.

Venison is often marinated until tender and served with a sauce of sweet raisins or red currants, or a purée of chestnuts. Try trout (*Forelle*)—this local fresh-water fish is unbeatable if boiled absolutely fresh (*blau*)—or some whitefish (*Renke*), usually fried.

Accompanying all meals is a crisp, green salad, or those familiar Bavarian staples, potato and cabbage. Choose from old standards such as sautéed potatoes (*Bratkartoffeln*) or try the excellent potato salad (*Kartoffelsalat*). Cabbage or *Sauerkraut* is often prepared in white wine with juniper berries, caraway seeds, and cloves. Also available is the sweet-and-sour red cabbage, or *Blaukraut*, cooked with apples, raisins, and white vinegar, or a good green cabbage salad (*Weisskrautsalat*).

Male waiters are called *Herr Ober* (hehr oaberr), female *Bedienung* (ber deenoong)

Snacks

Given the importance of beer-drinking within Munich's social life, snacks (*Schmankerl*) are correspondingly important both to aid and abet a thirst for beer, and to keep the drinkers "afloat," so to speak. You eat them at any time of day.

Local people enjoy sausages of all kinds as a snack food. Pork and veal join forces in the *Weisswürste* (white sausages), flavored with pepper, parsley, and onions. The best establishments—and in this case we mean those most observant of traditional standards—never serve *Weisswürste* in the afternoon. They are then no longer fresh enough for the discerning palate, which in this case is a Bavarian one. *Bratwurst*, another sausage staple, is made of pork and grilled or sautéed. The best are the little ones sent from Nuremberg. You should also enjoy the spicy *Blutwurst* (blood sausage) or *Leberwurst* (liver sausage).

Pretzels were invented by Bavarian brewers to soak up beer—and make you thirsty for more.

Also be on the look-out for a delicious snack with the misleading name of *Leberkäs*. Literally, this means "liver-cheese," but it contains neither liver nor cheese, being rather a mixture of pork, bacon, and beef, spiced with nutmeg, marjoram, and onions, eaten hot or cold. Other great snacks include: *Reiberdatschi*, or deep-fried potato pancakes; and *Obatzta*, a spicy mixture of creamy cheeses with chives, paprika, caraway seeds, salt and pepper, and thin slices of horseradish (*Radi*).

Failing any of these, you will always be able to stimulate your thirst with the salty pretzels (*Bretzel*).

Desserts

Apart from a couple of regional variations on apple cake (*Apfelküchert*) and plum cake (*Zwetschgendatschi*), Bavarians are quite content to join the rest of the country in the national obsession for *Konditorei* pastries. Other delicious treats offered in Bavaria are *Schwarzwälder Kirschtorte*, the cherry cake from the Black Forest, and *Apfelstrudel*.

Wines

Bavaria itself stopped making good wine some centuries ago, though the restaurants in Munich offer an excellent array of Rhine and Mosel wines, mostly white. Here's a guide to the best German vintages.

The Rhine wines with the highest reputation are those of the Rheingau, the pick of the crop being *Schloss Johannisberger*, *Hattenheimer*, *Kloster Eberbacher*, and *Rüdesheimer*. The next best come from the more southerly vineyards—the famous *Liebfraumilch*, *Niersteiner*, *Domtal*, and *Oppenheimer*, and next in quality are the Mittelrhein wines, coming from Bingen, Bacharach, Boppard, and Oberwesel.

Bier is practically served everywhere. Even some American fast food chains carry it.

The Mosel wines, bottled in green glass instead of the brown used for Rheingau wines, enjoy a reputation for delicacy, which has developed through the fame of the *Bernkasteler*, *Piesporter*, and *Zeltinger*.

Also produced in Germany is a very respectable sparkling, Champagne-like wine known as *Sekt*, from the Rheingau region of Eltville and Hochheim. (This latter region provides the English with their all-purpose term used to refer to German white wines, "hock.")

Beer

Bavarians endorse the old saying that there's good beer and better beer, but no bad beer. Especially not in Bavaria.

Bier vom Fass (on tap) can be ordered by the half-litre in restaurants, but elsewhere it is often only served in a one-litre tankard known as a *Masskrug* or simply *"Mass."* Bottled beer comes in several varieties: *Export* is light and smooth; *Pils* is light and strong; and *Bock* is dark and rich.

Bavarian beer is frequently lighter than the other German beers, but it has its strong varieties, too. If you like beer dark with a slightly sweet, malty flavor, order *Dunkles*. This is not served as cold as *Helles*, the more popular light lager brew, which is presented with an inviting mist on the glass.

Wherever you turn, there's beer. Pilsner-fueled people-watching is the rage in Viktualienmarkt.

Other Drinks

If you would rather be refreshed than stimulated, you'll find a wide assortment of fruit juices, the best of them being *Johannisbeersaft* (red or black currant), *Apfelsaft* (apple), *Orangensaft* (orange), and *Traubensaft* (non-alcoholic grape).

To Help You Order

Waiter/waitress, please!	**Ober/Fräulein, bitte.**
Could I/we have a table?	**Ich hätte/Wir hätten gerne einen Tisch.**

The check, please.	**Zahlen, bitte.**
I would like…	**Ich möchte gerne…**

beer	**ein Bier**	milk	**Milch**
bread	**etwas Brot**	mineral water	**Mineral-wasser**
butter	**etwas Butter**		
cheese	**Käse**	mustard	**etwas Senf**
coffee	**einen Kaffee**	potatoes	**Kartoffeln**
dessert	**eine Nachspeise**	salad	**Salat**
eggs	**Eier**	salt	**Salz**
fish	**Fisch**	soup	**eine Suppe**
hors d'œuvre	**eine Vorspeise**	tea	**einen Tee**
ice cream	**Eiskrem**	vegetables	**Gemüse**
meat	**Fleisch**	whipped cream	**Schlagsahne**
menu	**die Karte**	wine	**Wein**

…and Read the Menu

Apfel	apple	**Lachs**	salmon
Blumenkohl	cauliflower	**Lamm**	lamb
Braten	roast beef	**Nudeln**	noodles
Erdbeeren	strawberries	**Reis**	rice
Geselchtes	smoked meat	**Rindfleisch**	beef
Gurkensalat	cucumber salad	**Rippchen**	smoked pork chops
Hähnchen	chicken cutlet	**Schinken**	ham
Jäger-schnitzel	cutlet with mushroom sauce	**Schweine-fleisch**	pork
		Wild	game
Kalbfleisch	veal	**Wein**	wine
Kraftbrühe	bouillon	**Wurst**	sausage
Kraut	cabbage	**Zwiebeln**	onions
Krautwickerl	stuffed cabbage		

HANDY TRAVEL TIPS

An A–Z Summary of Practical Information

A

ACCOMMODATIONS (See also CAMPING, YOUTH HOSTELS, and the list of Recommended Hotels starting on page 127)

The Munich Tourist Offices provide a free multilingual list of accommodations in the city, with full details of amenities and prices. They also operate a hotel-booking service at the airport and at the central railway station for a small charge, and can help with queries (Tel. (089) 233 30 300; fax (089) 233 30 233). Part of the room rate must be paid in advance.

For a wider selection, consult the *German Hotel Guide,* distributed free by the German National Tourist Board. **The Allgemeine Deutsche Zimmerreservierung** (ADZ) operates a computer reservation system at Beethovenstrasse 61, D-60325 Frankfurt am Main, Tel. (069) 740 767.

In addition to hotels, there are inns (*Gasthof*) and boarding houses (*Pension*). The tourist office can arrange for accommodations in private homes — a nice way to get to know the local people. If you are touring Bavaria by car, look for "*Zimmer frei*" (room to rent) signs.

The Munich Tourist Office offers a special budget promotion, the "Munich Key." This package includes accommodations, a special ticket for all of Munich's public transport, and reductions on admission to museums, theaters, and other attractions. The Munich Key package can be booked at the Munich Tourist Offices at the central railway station and in the City Hall (see TOURIST INFORMATION OFFICES).

A list of hotels and inns in Upper Bavaria is available from **Fremdenverkehrsverband München-Bayern,** Prinzregentenstrasse 18, München 2, Tel. (089) 212 39 70.

I'd like a single room/ double room.	**Ich hätte gern ein Einzelzimmer/Doppelzimmer.**
with bath/shower	**mit Bad/Dusche**
What's the rate per night/week?	**Wieviel kostet es pro Nacht/Woche?**

AIRPORT *(Flughafen)*

Airport München Franz-Josef Straus, about 30 km (18 miles) east of the city center, handles domestic and international flights. You will find banks, car rental desks, restaurants, coffee bars, news- and souvenir-stands, a post office, hairdresser, hotel reservation desk, and duty-free shop. For flight information, Tel. (089) 97 521 313. Lufthansa (Germany's national airline) reservation desks can be reached by dialing (089) 545 599.

Ground transport: Taxis and suburban trains (S-Bahn) shuttle between the airport and the main railway station (Hauptbahnhof). The S-Bahn (S8) runs every 20 minutes between the airport and Pasing via the city center; the trip costs between DM 10 and 15. (The trains are equipped with places for luggage.) Tickets for the S-Bahn and U-Bahn should be purchased at the ticket kiosks at stations and in the airport. The trip takes between 28 and 45 minutes; the train station is outside the airport arrival hall (look for signs for the S-Bahn).

B

BUDGETING FOR YOUR TRIP

To give you an idea of what to expect, here's a list of average prices in marks (DM). They can only be approximate, however, as inflation creeps relentlessly up. The Munich Card, available from Tourist Offices, allows unlimited travel on all public transport and offers discounts of up to 50% on entry to major city attractions. It costs DM12 a day or DM29 for three days.

Airport transfer. S-Bahn line 8 to Central Train Station (Hauptbahnhof): DM10–15; taxi DM100.

Babysitters. DM15 per hour.

Camping. DM25–30 for two with car and tent or trailer.

Car rental. Some average examples include an *Opel Corsa 1.2*, DM95 per day, DM 450 per week with unlimited mileage; *Mercedes*

Benz C180 DM132 per day, DM700 per week with unlimited mileage. Tax included.

Cigarettes. DM4.50–5 per pack.

Entertainment. Cinema DM10–15, theater DM25–60, nightclub usually free, but you may have to buy a specified number of drinks.

Hotels (double room per night). Luxury class DM300–792, first class DM250–450, medium class DM180–370, budget class DM120–200. Boarding house DM80–150.

Meals and drinks. Continental breakfast DM10–20 (usually included in rate), lunch or dinner DM30–50, bottle of wine (German) DM30–40, beer (small) DM5–10, soft drinks (small) DM3, coffee DM4–6.

Museums. DM3–8.

MVV city transport. Day ticket, adults DM9 (one zone), DM18 (all zones), children DM3.20 (all zones). Single ticket DM1.90 (short journey), DM3.80 (one zone), each additional zone DM3.80. Strip tickets — adults DM16 (10-strip ticket), children DM6.50 (5-strip ticket).

Taxis. DM5, plus DM2.20 per km within center of Munich.

Youth hostels. Youth hostel (six-bed rooms) DM20–50 per person, breakfast included. Single rooms about DM50.

C

CAMPING

Four major campsites are situated within the city limits:

Langwieder See, Eschenrieder Strasse 119 (northwest, along the Augsburg-Stuttgart motorway), 81249 München, open April 1 to mid-October (Tel. (089) 864 15 66). Winter camping is available with advance registration.
Campingplatz **Nord-West** GmbH, Auf dem Schrederwiesen 3, 80995 München, open year-round (Tel. (089) 150 69 36).
München-**Obermenzing,** Lochhausener Strasse 59 (northwest, along the Augsburg-Stuttgart motorway), 81247 München, open mid-March to early November (Tel. (089) 811 22 35).
Campingplatz München-**Thalkirchen,** Zentralländstrasse 49

(on the Isar river, opposite the Zoo), 81379 München, open mid-March to end of October (Tel. (089) 723 17 07).

From the end of June through August, the city of Munich runs a campsite for young people, **Jugendlager Kapuzinerhölzl,** at Franz-Schrank-Strasse; Tel. (089) 514 106 16. A tent large enough for 300 people is set up; bring a sleeping bag and air mattress.

Sites are indicated by the international blue sign with a black tent on a white background. Some sites give reductions to members of the International Camping Association.

For full information about sites and facilities, consult the guides published by the German Automobile Club (**ADAC**) or the German Camping Club (**Deutscher Camping-Club — DCC**). You can contact DCC at: Mandlstrasse 28, D-80802 München 40; Tel. (089) 38 014 218. If you camp off the beaten track, be sure to obtain the permission of the proprietor or the police, and note that camping in the rest areas off the motorways is not permitted.

May we camp here?	**Dürfen wir hier zelten?**
Is there a campsite nearby?	**Gibt es in der Nähe einen Zeltplatz?**

CAR RENTAL *(Autovermietung)* (See also DRIVING)

You can arrange to rent a car immediately upon arrival at Munich's airport or central railway station. Otherwise inquire at your hotel or refer to the Yellow Pages of the telephone directory for addresses of leading firms. It's usually possible to have a car delivered to your hotel. Larger firms allow you to return cars to another European city for an extra fee. Special weekend and weekly unlimited mileage rates are usually available. Many airlines offer fly/drive packages to Munich, and the German Federal Railways promote a "Rail-and-Road" car rental program.

To rent a car you'll need to have held a valid driver's license for at least half a year; the minimum age is 19. If you do not pay by credit card you may have to pay a substantial cash deposit.

CLIMATE

Munich's climate can go to extremes, from the bitterest cold in winter to hot and either dry or muggy in summer. The dry, warm wind from the south, known as *Föhn,* can result in very clear, hot, dry conditions wonderful for visitors. Munich's average temperatures are given below.

	J	F	M	A	M	J	J	A	S	O	N	D
Daytime ° F	34	37	48	57	64	70	73	73	68	55	45	35
Daytime ° C	1	3	9	14	18	21	23	23	20	13	7	2

CLOTHING

During the winter months you'll need a heavy coat and warm clothing. In summer you should bring plenty of lightweight garments, and a bathing suit if you want to sunbathe or take a dip. A light wrap can come in handy for cool summer evenings. It may rain in spring and summer, so be prepared with a raincoat or umbrella.

At better hotels and restaurants, more formal clothes are expected, but there are few places where a tie is obligatory.

CRIME and SAFETY (See also EMERGENCIES and POLICE)

Compared to most urban centers, Munich's crime rate is quite low. Nonetheless it's advisable to take all the normal precautions. Don't leave money or valuables in your car or hotel room; lock them in the hotel safe instead. If you are robbed, report the incident to the hotel receptionist and the nearest police station. The police will provide you with a certificate to present to your insurance company, or to your consulate if your passport has been stolen.

I want to report a theft.	**Ich möchte einen Diebstahl melden.**
My handbag/wallet/ passport has been stolen.	**Meine Handtasche/ Brieftasche/mein Pass ist gestohlen worden.**

CUSTOMS *(Zoll)* and ENTRY REGULATIONS

For a stay of up to three months, a valid passport is sufficient for citizens of Australia, Canada, New Zealand, South Africa, and the United States. Visitors from the Irish Republic and the United Kingdom need only an identity card to enter Germany.

As Germany is part of the European Union, the free exchange of non-duty-free goods for personal use is permitted between Germany, the UK, and the Irish Republic (residents only). For non-European residents, and for goods bought duty-free within Europe and the EU, the restrictions on import into Germany are as follows: 200 cigarettes or 50 cigars or 250*g* tobacco, and 1*l* of spirits or 2*l* of wine (including fortified wines).

Restrictions for visitors from outside Europe on returning to their home country are as follows: **Australia,** 250*g* tobacco products and 1 litre of alcoholic beverages; **Canada,** 200 cigarettes and 50 cigars and 400*g* tobacco, 1.14*l* of liquor or wine or 8.5*l* of beer; **USA,** 200 cigarettes and 100 cigars and a reasonable amount of tobacco, 1 US quart of alcoholic beverages.

Currency restrictions. There are no restrictions on the import or export of marks or any other currency.

I've nothing to declare.	**Ich habe nichts zu verzollen.**
It's for personal use.	**Es ist für meinen persönlichen Gebrauch.**

D

DRIVING in MUNICH

To bring your car into Germany you will need: a national (or international for those coming from the US, Australia, or South Africa) driver's license; car registration papers; a national identity car sticker; a red warning triangle in case of breakdown; and a first-aid kit.

Insurance. Third-party insurance is compulsory. Visitors have to present their international insurance certificate (Green Card) or take out third-party insurance at the German border. For EU visitors, the green card is no longer compulsory but is strongly recommended.

Seat belts are obligatory for front-seat *and* back-seat passengers if the car is so equipped. If you don't wear them, insurance companies will reduce compensation in the event of an accident.

Driving conditions. Traffic jams, a lack of parking space, pedestrian areas, and one-way streets all make driving in Munich a frustrating experience. It's far better to get around town by the public transport system, which is excellent — the tourist office provides a brochure listing points of interest and detailing how to get there by bus or underground. Bear in mind that bottlenecks form on major approach roads into Munich at the beginning and end of peak holiday periods.

Drive on the right, pass on the left. On the *Autobahn* (motorway, expressway), passing another vehicle on the right is prohibited; cars with trailers are not allowed to pass on certain stretches (watch for signs); and should police or emergency vehicles need to pass through a traffic jam (*Stau*), cars in the right lane must keep close to the right, and those in the left lane close to the left, thereby opening a passageway down the middle. In the absence of traffic lights, or stop or yield signs, vehicles coming from the right have priority at intersections, unless otherwise indicated. At traffic circles, approaching cars must give way to traffic already in the circle, unless otherwise indicated. Trams must be passed on the right and never at a stop (unless there's a traffic island).

At dusk, and in case of bad visibility, headlights or dipped headlights must be used; driving with parking lights only is forbidden, even in built-up areas.

Speed limits. The speed limit is 100 km/h (62 mph) on all open roads except for motorways and divided highways, where there's no limit unless otherwise indicated (the suggested maximum speed is 130 km/h, or 81 mph). In town, the limit is 50 km/h (31 mph), except on the Mittlerer Ring, the six-lane ring road system around the city, where the limit is 60km/h (37mph). Cars towing trailers may not exceed 80 km/h (50 mph).

Traffic police (see also POLICE) may confiscate the car keys of persons they consider unfit to drive. Drinking and driving is a very serious offense in Germany. The permissible level of alcohol in the blood is 0.8 per mille (millilitres), or about two glasses of beer. Be careful, too, to stay within speed limits; the police are getting more and more strict, and radar is used both inside and out of towns.

Breakdowns. In the event of a breakdown on the Autobahn and other important roads, use one of the emergency telephones located every second kilometre (the direction of the nearest one is indicated by a small arrow on the reflector poles at the roadside). Ask for Strassenwacht, run jointly by the two German automobile clubs ADAC and AvD. Assistance is free; towing and spare parts have to be paid for. For round-the-clock breakdown service, call (0180) 222 22 22.

Fuel and oil *(Benzin; Öl)*. Service stations are everywhere, many of them self-service. It's usual to tip attendants for any extra attention.

Fluid measures

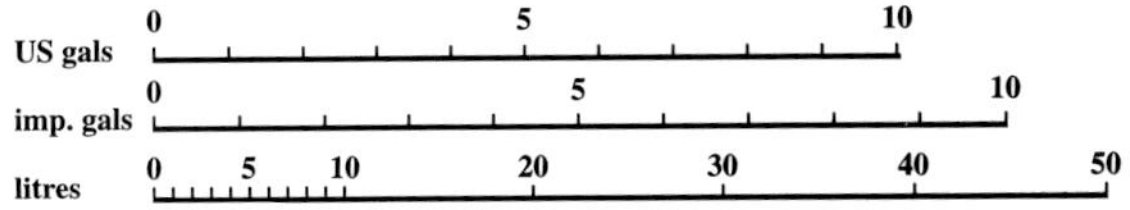

Road signs. Most road signs employed in Germany are international pictographs, but here are some written ones you might come across:

One-way street	**Einbahnstrasse**
Get into lane	**Einordnen**
Pedestrians	**Fussgänger**
Short-term parking	**Kurzparkzone**
Keep left	**Links fahren**
No parking	**Parken verboten**
Men working	**Strassenarbeiten**
Detour	**Umleitung**
Caution	**Vorsicht**
(Internationaler) Führerschein	(International) Driver's License

Kraftfahrzeugpapiere	Car Registration Papers
Grüne Karte	Green Card
Wo ist der nächste Parkplatz?	Where's the nearest parking lot?
Bitte volltanken.	Full tank, please.
Super/bleifreies Benzin/Diesel	Super/lead-free/diesel
Kontrollieren Sie bitte das Öl/die Reifen/die Batterie.	Check the oil/tires/battery, please.
Ich habe eine Panne.	I've had a breakdown.
Es ist ein Unfall passiert.	There's been an accident.

E

ELECTRIC CURRENT

Germany has 220-volt, 50-cycle AC. Plugs are the standard Continental type for which British and North American appliances need an adapter.

EMBASSIES and CONSULATES *(Konsulat)*

Canada	Tal 29, Munich 2; Tel. (089) 219 95 70.
Irish Republic	Mauerkircherstrasse la, Munich 80; Tel. (089) 985 723-25.
South Africa	Sendlinger-Tor-Platz 5, Munich 2; Tel. (089) 231 16 30.
UK	Burkleinstrasse 10, Munich 22; Tel. (089) 211 090.
US	Königinstrasse 5, Munich 22; Tel. (089) 288 80.

EMERGENCIES (See also EMBASSIES AND CONSULATES, DRIVING, MEDICAL CARE, and POLICE)

Emergency telephone numbers:

Police:	**110**
Fire:	**112**

Ambulance:	**19222**

If you don't speak German, try English, or ask the first person you see to help you call.

There is an emergency helpline for victims of sexual violence (including rape), Tel. 763 737.

Please, can you place an emergency call for me to the…?	**Würden Sie bitte… für mich anrufen?**
police/fire brigade/hospital	**die Polizei/die Feuer wehr/das Krankenhaus**

G

GAY and LESBIAN TRAVELERS (see also WOMEN)

Munich has an open atmosphere and is very accepting of all lifestyles. In particular, there is an area around the theater district called Görtnerplatz where there are many gay restaurants and clubs. "Our Munich" is a monthly gay and lesbian city guide.

Schwules Kommunikations und Kulturzentrum, Müllerstrasse 43, Tel. (089) 260 30 56.
Counseling for Lesbians, Tel. (089) 725 42 72 (English-speaking service available).

GETTING THERE (see also AIRPORT)

A good travel agent can give you up-to-date information on the wide range of fares, package holidays, or short breaks currently available.

By air. Flughafen München Franz Josef Strauss is served by many European and about 90 intercontinental flights a day. However, the main airport for transatlantic flights is still Frankfurt, from where there are several flights a day to Munich. Average travel time from London to Munich is 1½ hours, from New York 9 hours.

By car. Munich can be reached by motorway (expressway) from nearly anywhere in Europe (Brussels–Munich 815 km/505 miles, Basel 394 km/244 miles, Hamburg 795 km/493 miles).

By coach. Tour operators in Germany and abroad offer coach tours to Munich all year round. Seats must be booked in advance. London to Munich direct takes approximately 24 hours.

By rail. Information on trains and reduced-price tickets is on page 120. There are numerous trains daily from London to Munich via Dover and Ostend, a journey of 17 hours. The day-service via Harwich and the Hook of Holland (20 hours) is direct, but passengers on the night train must change in Cologne. Through the summer months there's a *Train Auto Couchettes* from Paris to Munich. Seats or sleepers should be booked well in advance.

GUIDES and TOURS

The tourist office will put you in touch with qualified guides and interpreters if you want a personally conducted tour or if you need linguistic assistance. City sightseeing tours by bus start from opposite the main entrance of the central railway station, in front of the Hertie department store. Daily excursions by coach to outlying towns and villages are also organized: inquire at the tourist office for details, or at the Panorama Tours office, Arnulfstrasse 8, 80355 München; Tel. (089) 550 289 95; fax (089) 549 075 70.

H

HEALTH and MEDICAL CARE (See also EMERGENCIES)

If you already have private medical insurance, find out whether or not you are covered for medical treatment in Germany. Visitors who are not covered can take out a short-term holiday policy before setting out.

Citizens of European Union countries are eligible for free medical treatment, and should obtain the requisite form from their Health and Social Security Office prior to their departure. However it is still advisable to take out holiday insurance; a reputable policy will provide far more comprehensive coverage in the case of serious illness or accident.

In an emergency call for an ambulance (**19 222**). If you require medical attention you can contact the American or British consulates for a list of English-speaking doctors and dentists.

Pharmacies are open during normal shopping hours. At night, on Sundays, and on holidays, all pharmacies display the address of the nearest one open. For the Pharmacy emergency service call **59 44 75**.

It is perfectly safe to drink the tap water in Germany; only rarely will you see the sign "Kein Trinkwasser" (which means "not drinking water," usually at public squares and in trains). If you order water in restaurants you will automatically be served fizzy mineral water. If this is not what you want you should order *stilles Mineralwasser* (natural Mineral water).

No vaccinations are required for entry to Germany.

Where's the nearest (all-night) pharmacy?	**Wo ist die nächste diensthabende Apotheke?**
I need a doctor/dentist.	**Ich brauche einen Arzt/Zahnarzt.**
I have a pain here.	**Ich habe hier Schmerzen.**
stomachache	**Magenschmerzen**
headache	**Kopfschmerzen**
a fever	**Fieber**
medical emergency service	**Ärztlicher Notdienst**
ambulance	**Rettungsdienst**
hospital	**Krankenhaus**

HOLIDAYS *(Feiertag)*

On public holidays, shops, banks, offices, and many restaurants are closed. If a holiday falls on a Thursday, it may turn into a long weekend. On 24 and 31 December, shops are open until midday.

Most restaurants, theaters, cinemas, and concert halls close on Christmas Eve.

Fixed Holidays:

1 Jan	*Neujahr*	New Year's Day
6 Jan	*Heilige Drei Könige*	Epiphany
1 May	*Tag der Arbeit*	Labor Day
15 Aug	*Mariä Himmelfahrt*	Assumption Day
3 Oct	*Tag der Deutschen Einheit*	Day of National Unity
1 Nov	*Allerheiligen*	All Saints' Day
25-26 Dec	*Weihnachten*	Christmas

Movable Holidays:

Karfreitag	Good Friday
Ostermontag	Easter Monday
Christi Himmelfahrt	Ascension Day
Pfingstmontag	Whit Monday
Fronleichnam	Corpus Christi
Buss- und Bettag	Day of Repentance (3rd Wednesday in November)

I

INTERNET and E-MAIL

Many hotels offer e-mail facilities to their guests. In addition, there are several Internet cafés in the city. These include Times Square Online Bistro, Bayer Strasse 10a, which is open daily from 6:30am–1am; Internet Café, Altheimer Eck 12 (open daily 11am–1am); and Internet Café, Nymphenburger Strasse 145 (open daily 11am–4am).

L

LANGUAGE

About one-third of the Munich population speaks a form of Bavarian dialect. Real Bavarian is difficult to understand, even for the many northern Germans who live in Munich; but Bavarians can often be persuaded to speak something closer to standard German. English is widely understood and spoken, and most of the larger shops have English-speaking staff, but don't take it for granted.

Do you speak English? **Sprechen Sie Englisch?**

LOST PROPERTY

Munich's general lost-property office, Fundbüro der Stadtverwaltung, is at Oetztalerstrasse 17 (Tel. (089) 233 459 01)

For property lost on trains, contact the *Fundbüro* at the central railway station (Tel. 089/13 08 66 44), if it is within three days of the loss. Otherwise, contact the main lost-property offices of the Bundesbahn, at Landsbergerstr. 472; Tel. (089) 130 858 59. The S-Bahn lost-property office is at the east railway station (*Ostbahnhof*), Tel. (089) 130 844 09.

I've lost my wallet/my bag/my passport. **Ich habe meine Brieftasche/meine Tasche/ meinen Pass verloren.**

M

MEDIA

Newspapers and magazines *(Zeitung; Zeitschrift)*. Major British, American, and Continental newspapers and magazines are on sale at newsstands in the city center, as well as at larger hotels, the central railway station, and the airport. A monthly guide in German to upcoming events (*Monatsprogramm*) is available at the tourist office, hotels and newsstands. *Munich Found*, Bavaria's monthly entertainment magazine in English, is available at kiosks and bookstores. There are two English bookshops in Schellingstrasse, near the university.

Have you any English-language newspapers? **Haben Sie Zeitungen in englischer Sprache?**

Radio and TV (*Radio; Fernsehen*). You can easily pick up the BBC World Service, American Forces Network (AFN), or the

Voice of America. The Bavarian Radio Service (*Bayerischer Rundfunk*) has the news daily in English. There are two national television channels — ARD (Channel One) and ZDF (Channel Two) — a regional station, *Drittes Programm,* and numerous private channels. Films are sometimes shown in the original English version, and a news bulletin is relayed in English once a week. Many hotels carry CNN, BBC World, CNBC, and other English-language channels.

MONEY MATTERS (See also CUSTOMS AND ENTRY REGULATIONS)

Currency. Germany's monetary unit is the Deutsche Mark (DM). The mark is divided into 100 Pfennig (Pf). Coins: 1, 2, 5, 10, and 50 Pf. and DM 1, 2, and 5. Notes: DM 5, 10, 20, 50, 100, 500, and 1,000.

ATMs. ATMs are located throughout the city. Many offer cash withdrawal for Visa, Mastercard, American Express, Cirrus, or Plus cards. Be sure to know your PIN for cash withdrawals on credit cards.

Banks and currency exchange. Foreign currency can be changed at ordinary banks (*Bank*), savings banks (*Sparkasse*), and currency exchange offices (*Wechselstube*). It can also be changed at hotels, travel agencies, and Munich's central post office, but rates are not as good. Money can be changed at the central railway station from 6am to 11pm every day, or at the main post office 24 hours a day. Always take your passport with you to change money or travelers' checks.

Credit cards are accepted in most major hotels and many restaurants, shops, and major service stations.

Travelers' checks and eurocheques are welcome almost everywhere. Eurocheques are particularly widely used.

I want to change some pounds/dollars.	**Ich möchte Pfund/Dollars wechseln.**
Do you accept travelers' checks?	**Nehmen Sie Reiseschecks?**
Can I pay with this credit card?	**Kann ich mit dieser Kreditkarte zahlen?**

O

OPEN HOURS (See also HOLIDAYS)

Banks are usually open from 8:30am–12:30pm and 1:30–3:30pm, Monday–Friday (Thursday until 5:30pm). Some bigger banks in the city center remain open during lunch hour. Banks at the airport operate daily from about 7am until around 9pm. Transactions can also be made at the central railway station daily from 6am–11pm.

Museum hours vary, but are usually from 9:30am to 5 or 6pm. Most museums close on Mondays. (See page 56 for further details.)

Restaurants in the city center often stay open all day. Breakfast is until 10am, lunch from noon–2:30pm, and dinner from 6–11pm.

Shops are generally open from 8:30 or 9am–8:30pm, Monday–Friday, and till 4pm (some till 12:30) on Saturdays. Shops outside the city center usually close between 1 and 3pm.

P

PHOTOGRAPHY

Some of the world's best cameras come from Germany, so you may want to get equipped here. All brands of film are available. Developing usually takes 1–2 days; some shops provide overnight service.

Most modern security machines will not ruin your film; if in doubt ask, or pass films through separately.

Videos in Germany use the PAL system (not NTSC), so make sure that your system is compatible with any videos you buy. You can get videos copied from PAL to NTSC in Munich or when you get home.

I'd like a roll of film.	**Ich hätte gern einen Film.**
black-and-white film/color film	**Schwarzweissfilm/Farbfilm**
How long will it take to develop this film?	**Wie lange dauert das Entwickeln?**

POLICE *(Polizei)* (See also EMERGENCIES)

Germany's police wear green uniforms. You'll see them on white motorcycles or in green-and-white cars. Street parking in towns is supervised by police officers in dark-blue uniforms. If you are fined, they have the right to ask you to pay on the spot.

The police emergency number is **110;** the Fire Department is **112.** Munich's central police station (*Polizeipräsidium*) is at Ettstrasse 2.

Where's the nearest police station?	**Wo ist die nächste Polizeiwache?**

POST OFFICES

Munich's central post office is in the main train station (Hauptbahnhof). It is open Monday–Friday, 7am–8pm, Saturday 8am–4pm, Sunday and holidays 9am–3pm. Most post offices are open from 8am to 6pm, Monday to Friday (till noon on Saturdays). They also handle telegrams and telephone calls.

Mailboxes are painted yellow with a black post-horn. Stamps can be purchased at yellow vending machines near mailboxes and at some tobacconists and stationers.

Poste restante (general delivery). This service is taken care of by Munich's central post office: If you have mail addressed to you c/o Hauptpostlagernd, it will arrive at the central post office. Be sure to always take your passport or identity card when you go to collect your mail.

A stamp for this letter/ postcard, please.	**Eine Briefmarke für diesen Brief/diese Karte, bitte.**
express (special delivery)	**Eilzustellung**
airmail	**Luftpost**
registered	**Eingeschrieben**
Have you received any mail for…?	**Ist Post da für…?**
I want to send a telegram to…	**Ich möchte ein telegramm nach… aufgeben.**

PUBLIC TRANSPORTATION

Munich is served by an efficient network of buses, trams, U-Bahn (underground railway), and S-Bahn (suburban railway, a part of the German Federal Railways). The U- and S-Bahn serve the city center, while the S-Bahn goes out to suburbs and the surrounding countryside. All forms of public transport operate from about 5am to 1am daily. Free maps and information are available at the tourist offices.

Tickets, interchangeable between U-Bahn, S-Bahn, buses, and trams, entitle you to free transfers for up to two hours so long as you travel in the same direction. Buy your tickets from the big blue vending machines at U- and S-Bahn stations (or on buses and at tram stops, hotels, tobacconists, newsagents, and stationers that display a white "K"). Vending machines are marked *Einzelfahrkarte* (single ticket) or *Streifenenkarte* (strip ticket). The strip tickets work out cheaper if you intend to make several trips. Be sure to cancel tickets in the blue canceling machines positioned at platform entrances and in buses and trams; if you have a strip ticket you need to cancel **two** strips per zone traveled (children cancel only one strip per zone).

Make sure you keep your ticket handy while you are using the public transit system, in case of spot checks.

The Munich Welcome Card offers an excellent way to make significant savings in public transport costs, together with providing reductions in entry prices for many of the city's major museums and attractions. Holders of the card, which is available from the Tourist Offices, are entitled to unlimited use of public transport throughout the metropolitan area. A single Day Ticket costs DM12, a Single Three Day Ticket, which is valid for 72 hours, costs DM29, and a Partner Three Day Ticket, which is valid for 72 hours and covers up to five people, costs DM42.

Taxis. Munich taxis are beige in color. Catch one at a taxi stand, as it's not common practice to hail a taxi in the street. During rush hour, it is wise to book in advance, through your hotel receptionist or by phoning Tel. (089) 216 10, (089) 194 10, or (089) 450 540.

Intercity bus services. Rural areas are served by the Federal Railways (Bundesbahn) buses and the Federal Post Office (Bundespost) buses, as well as local companies. In Munich, the bus terminal is in Arnulfstrasse, in the front of Starnberg Station (on the north side of the central railway station).

Trains. Deutsche Bahn (German Rail) trains are extremely comfortable and fast, as well as punctual. EC (Euro City) are international trains; IC (Inner City) and ICE (Inter City Express) are long-distance national trains. The ICE trains are very fast, reaching speeds of up to 280 kph (174 mph), and feature restaurants and aircraft-like video screens on some seats. IR (InterRegio) trains run every hour between major cities, and RE (Regional Express) are local trains that make only limited stops.

Reduced price offers and bargain tickets are available.

Eurail passes (these rail tickets covering Western Europe are only available to those living outside of Europe, and must be bought before you arrive in Europe); Euro Domino, allowing unlimited travel in Germany for any three to eight days within one month; the Bahncard — suitable for frequent travelers in Germany, this allows discounts of 50% off the regular fare for all train journeys in the country over a one-year period. Detailed information is available in English from the International Visitors section of the Deutsche Bahn web site <www.bahn.de> or by calling Deutsche Bahn UK Booking Centre in England, Tel. (0870) 24 35 363.

For further details, ask at travel agencies, German National Tourist offices in your home country, or DB railway offices.

Hitchhiking. This is forbidden only on the Autobahn. However, if you try thumbing a lift, you'll be lucky if anyone stops for you.

Car-share groups. Some associations arrange intercity trips (*Mitfahrgelegenheiten*); try the following addresses:

Mitfahrzentrale, Lämmerstr. 4, Tel. (089) 194 40; fax (089) 594 564.

Citynetz Mitfahrzentrale Kangursh, Adalbertstrasse 10–12, Tel. (089) 194 44; fax (089) 330 400 68.
There are fixed-price tickets for the journeys, according to the distance, and for a small fee you can also have insurance coverage.

When's the next bus/train to …?	**Wann fährt der nächste Bus/Zug nach…?**
I want a ticket to …	**Ich möchte eine Fahrkarte nach…**
one-way (single)	**einfach**
round-trip (return)	**hin und zurück**
first/second class	**erste/zweite Klasse**

R

RELIGION

Almost half of the Munich population is Roman Catholic and about one-third Protestant. There is also a large Jewish community.

Several church services are held in English for different denominations, such as: St. Bonifaz, Karlstrasse; Kreuzkirche, Kreuzstrasse (Roman Catholic), and Seybothstrasse 4 (Anglican-Episcopal). For times of these — and other — services, refer to the monthly guide *Monatsprogramm*, or call (089) 11 57.

T

TELEPHONE

Avoid placing calls through your hotel, as the fee is likely to be considerably higher than in a phone booth. Telephone booths, glass boxes with gray or yellow frames, bear a sign showing a black receiver in a yellow square (national calls) or a green square (national and international calls). Area code numbers are listed in a special telephone book. Communications within Germany and to neighboring countries are cheaper after 9pm weekdays and all day Saturdays, Sundays, and public holidays. Telephone cards for DM12 or DM50 can be purchased at the post office.

Many international phone services have access numbers inside Germany, so it is possible to charge international calls to a domestic phone card.

Some useful numbers:

Inquiries: domestic **11 833** international **11 834**

Can I use the telephone?	**Kann ich das Telefon benutzen?**
Can you get me this number in …	**Können Sie mich mit dieser Nummer in … verbinden?**
collect call (reverse-charge)	**R-Gespräch**
person-to-person (personal) call	**Gespräch mit Voranmeldung**

TIME ZONES

Germany follows Central European Time (GMT + 1). In summer, the clock is put one hour ahead (GMT + 2):

New York	London	**Munich**	Jo'burg	Sydney	Auckland
6am	11am	**noon**	noon	8pm	10pm

What time is it, please? **Wie spät ist es, bitte?**

TIPPING

Since a service charge is normally included in hotel and restaurant bills, tipping is not obligatory, but is widely practiced. It's appropriate to give something extra to bellboys and coat-check attendants for their services. Below are some suggestions as to how much to leave.

Porter, per bag	DM1
Maid, per week	DM5–10
Lavatory attendant	DM0.30–.50
Waiter	optional (round off)
Taxi driver	round off
Hairdresser/Barber	10–15%
Tour guide	10%

TOILETS

Public toilets are easily found: museums, all restaurants, bars, cafés, large stores, airports, and railway stations provide facilities. If there's an attendant, and hand towels and soap are offered, you should leave a small tip. Always have several 10-Pfennig coins ready in case the door has a coin-operated latch. Toilets may be labeled with symbols of a man or a woman or the initials *W. C.* Otherwise *Herren* (Gentlemen) and *Damen* (Ladies) or a double zero (00) sign are indicated.

Where are the toilets, please?	**Wo sind die Toiletten, bitte?**

TOURIST INFORMATION OFFICES

The German National Tourist Board — Deutsche Zentrale für Tourismus (DZT) — can inform you about when to go, where to stay and what to see in Munich: **DZT,** Beethovenstrasse 69, D-60325 Frankfurt am Main, Tel. (069) 974 640, fax (069) 751 903.

The national tourist organization also maintains offices in many countries throughout the world:

Canada:	175 Bloor Street East, North Tower, Suite 604, Toronto, Ont. M4W 3R8; Tel. (416) 968-1570; fax (416) 968-1986.
UK:	P.O. Box 2695, London W1A 3TN; Tel. 0207 317 0908; fax 0207 495 6125.
US:	122 East 42nd Street, New York, NY 10168; Tel. (212) 661-7200; fax (212) 661 7174.
	11766 Wilshire Boulevard, Suite 750, Los Angeles, CA 90025, Tel. (310) 575-9799.
	401 North Michigan Avenue, Suite 2525, Chicago, IL 60611-4212; Tel. (312) 644-0723; fax (312) 644 0724).

Munich's Tourist Offices are located at the Main Train Station, Bahnhofsplatz 2, Tel. (089) 233 302 57 (open Monday–Saturday 9am–8pm and Sundays and holidays 10am–6pm), and in the City

Hall, Marienplatz, Tel. (089) 233 302 72 (open Monday–Friday 10am–8pm and Saturday 10am–4pm).

Address inquiries to:
Fremdenverkehrsamt München, Postfach 80313 München; fax (089) 23 33 02 33; e-mail <tourismus@muenchen.btl.de>.

Munich Tourist offices offer a hotel booking service for a small fee. The official Monatsprogramm of events is on sale there, as is the Munich Card. You can also listen to recorded information in English for museums and galleries: Tel. (089) 233 300 70.

For information about Bavaria, contact the Munich–Upper Bavaria Tourist Association at the following address: Fremdenverkehrsverband München-Bayern, Prinzregentenstrasse 18, 80538 Muenchen, Tel. (089) 212 39 70.

TRAVELERS with DISABILITIES

Munich is a very accessible city, with most large hotels, museums, and public transport equipped with ramps, elevators, and special access. It's advisable to check at smaller places before you go.

In the hotel section of this guide we have noted which hotels have particularly good facilities or special rooms for wheelchair users. Contact the hotel for more detailed information.

City guides are available to accompany visitors with disabilities; call (089) 356 88 08 Tuesday and Thursday 6 to 8pm.

Munich's central post office, opposite the station, has write-read phones available for the hearing-impaired from 7am to 11pm.

W

WEB SITES

A great deal of information about Munich can be obtained from the Internet. The Tourist Office and many hotels have their own sites. Some useful addresses of English-language sites include:

<www.munich-tourist.de> This is the English-language site of the Munich Tourist Board.

<www.munichfound.com> This online version of the Tourist Board's handy Visitor's Guide is in English.

<www.munich-online.de> This German-language site is still useful, even if you don't speak German, as it contains information about upcoming events, etc.

WEIGHTS and MEASURES

Distance

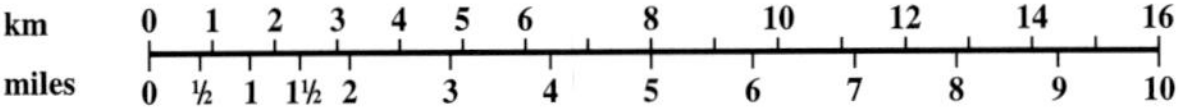

Length

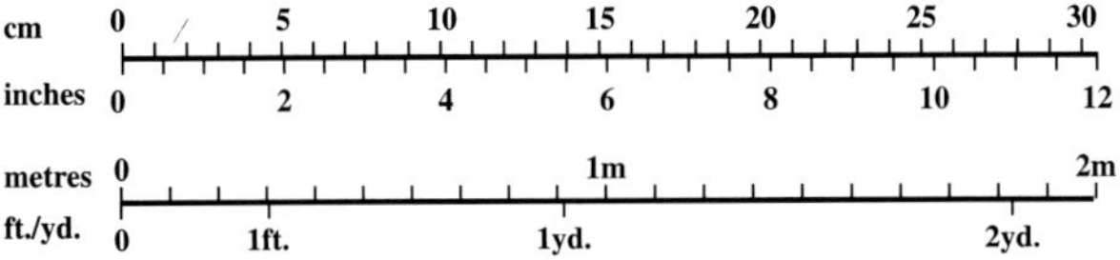

Weight

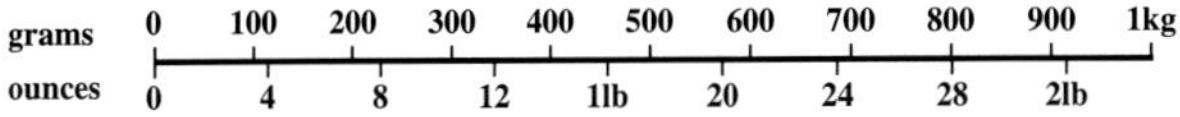

Munich uses the metric system. See DRIVING IN MUNICH on page 107 for fluid measurement conversions.

WOMEN (see also EMERGENCIES, GAY AND LESBIAN TRAVELERS, and PUBLIC TRANSPORTATION)

An extraordinary number and variety of organizations in the city of Munich cater specifically to women. You can find a full listing in the local publication, *Monatsprogramm*. It is advisable to check the opening times of the following organizations before you visit, as their hours may change from season to season.

24-hour help and advice for women: (089) 354 830, (089) 354 83 11.

Women-only guarded parking lots: Rosenheimer Str. 5, open 8am to 12am, St-Jakobs-Platz, Oberanger 35-37, open 24 hours.

Frauenkulturhaus (women's cultural center), Richard Strauss Str. 21, Tel. (089) 47 052 12.

Frauentreffpunkt Neuperlach (meeting point, café), Oskar Maria Graf Ring 20/22, Tel. (089) 67 064 63.

Lillemor's Frauenbuchladen (women's bookshop), Arcisstr. 57, Tel. (089) 27 212 05.

Y

YOUTH HOSTELS

If you are planning to make extensive use of youth hostels during your stay in Munich, obtain an international membership card from your national youth hostel association. For full information about hostels in Germany, contact the German Youth Hostel Association (Deutsches Jugendherbergswerk — DJH), Bülowstrasse 26, D-32756 Detmold, Tel. (05231) 7401-0. The following hostels are located in and around Munich:

Christlicher Verein Junger Männer (YMCA), Landwehrstrasse 13, 80336 München, Tel. (089) 552 141 0; fax (089) 550 42 82.

DJH Jugendgästehaus München, Miesingstrasse 4, Tel. (089) 723 65 50; fax (089) 724 25 67; e-mail <BineMunich@aol.com>.

Haus International Jugendhotel, Elisabethstrasse 87, 80797 München (Schwabing), Tel. (089) 120 060; fax (089) 120 06 251.

Recommended Hotels

Choosing a hotel in a city that you're not familiar with can be daunting; in this section we have selected a range of tried-and-trusted hotels to get you started. There are hotel-booking facilities at the main tourist information offices in Munich (see ACCOMMODATIONS on page 102, and TOURIST INFORMATION OFFICES on page 123). For a short stay it is worth considering "Munich Key" budget packages, which are of particularly good value and provide all you need for your visit to the city, including maps and public transport vouchers. Contact the Munich Tourist Offices for more information.

We have arranged the hotels under headings according to geographical location; Innenstadt, or Inner city; West of Karlstor, the area near the main railway station; Theresienwiese, near the Oktoberfest site and exhibition grounds; Isar for hotels east of the inner city near the riverbanks; and Schwabing, north of the city center.

We have also included a small selection of hotels in the areas covered in our Excursions section, near the Starnberger See and Ludwig's Follies.

The symbols below are a guide to the price of a standard double room with bathroom. Breakfast may be extra. Many hotels in Munich supply breakfast only, no restaurant meals. These hotels are listed as B&B only. All prices are inclusive of service and tax.

$$$$	Above DM400
$$$	DM280–400
$$	DM200–280
$	Below DM200

INNENSTADT

Adler $ *Ledererstr. 8; Tel. (089) 223 99 12; fax (089) 228 94 37.* Central location near Alter Hof and Toy Museum. Parking available. 60 beds.

Advokat $$ *Baaderstrasse 1, 80469 Munich; Tel. (089) 21 63 10; fax (089) 21 63 190; email <info@hotel-advocat.de>.* Stylish hotel with modern interior design, located in the fashionable Gärnerplatz district, just five minutes' walk from Marienplatz. Excellent breakfast buffet. 50 rooms.

Bayerischer Hof $$$$ *Promenadepl. 2–6; Tel. (089) 21 200; fax (089) 21 20 906; e-mail <hbh@compuserve.com>.* Luxury hotel in the beautiful Palais Mongelas; full facilities, including garage, bars and restaurants, roof-top garden, swimming pool, sauna, and shops. Wheelchair access. 409 rooms.

Daniel $ *am Stachus, Sonnenstr. 5; Tel. (089) 54 82 40; fax (089) 55 34 20; e-mail <info@Hotel-Daniel.de>.* Comfortable, friendly hotel in a central location just off the Karlsplatz, not far from the station. 75 rooms, B&B only.

Hotel Exquisit $$$ *Pettenkoferstrasse 3, 80336 Munich; Tel. (089) 551 99 00; fax (089) 551 99 499.* Comfortable hotel located close to Sendlinger Tor, a 10-minute walk from Marienplatz. Good buffet breakfast. Sauna, solarium, garden terrace. Disabled access. 50 rooms.

Platzl Hotel $$$$ *Sparkassenstrasse 10; Tel. (089) 23 7030; fax (089) 23 703 800.* Bavarian-style hotel in the heart of Munich near the Marienplatz; parking, restaurant and bar, conference rooms, jacuzzi, fitness room, sauna, and solarium. Wheelchair access. 270 beds.

Schlicker $–$$ *Tal 8; Tel. (089) 22 79 41; fax (089) 29 60 59; e-mail <schlicker-munich@t-online.de>.* Simple hotel with few facilities, but situated in the heart of Munich near the Marienplatz. Car access and parking available. 120 beds, B&B only.

WEST of KARLSTOR

Alfa $ *Hirtenstr. 22; Tel. (089) 545 95 30; fax (089) 545 95 3299; e-mail <empfang@hotel-alfa.de>.* Conveniently situated near the station, but in a quiet side-street location. Garage and other parking available. 77 rooms, B&B only.

City Hotel $$ *Schillerstr. 3a; Tel. (089) 55 80 91; fax (089) 550 36 65.* Modern hotel with air-conditioning, parking, and restaurant. 65 rooms.

Deutsches Theater $$ *Landwehrstrasse 18, 80336 Munich; Tel. (089) 545 85 25; fax (089) 545 85 261.* Relaxed, privately-run hotel in a central location. All 27 rooms are decorated with Laura Ashley-style fabrics.

Eden-Hotel Wolff $–$$ *Arnulfstr. 4–8; Tel. (089) 55 11 50; fax (089) 55 11 5555.* Opposite main station, near city center. Spacious and comfortable rooms, tasteful decoration, all windows sound-proofed. Café, bar, good restaurant serving Bavarian food, shop, banquet halls, and conference rooms available. Garage. 220 rooms.

Europäischer Hof $–$$ *Bayerstr. 31; Tel. (089) 55 15 10; fax (089) 55 15 1222; e-mail <info@heh.de>.* Comfortable hotel with all windows sound-proofed, Italian restaurant, conference rooms, and parking. 153 rooms.

Intercity Hotel $$ *Bayerstr. 10; Tel. (089) 54 55 60; fax (089) 545 566 10; e-mail <reservierung@intercity-hotel.de>.* Modern, elegant hotel, decorated in alpine style, with comfortable rooms, sound-proofed windows, restaurants and bars, conference rooms, and a bowling alley. Good wheelchair access. 203 rooms.

Mercure City $$ *Senefelderstr. 9; Tel. (089) 55 13 20; fax (089) 59 64 44; e-mail <HO878@accor-hotels.com>.* High-class hotel situated near the main station, only minutes' walk from the exhibition grounds, with 5 conference rooms, restaurant, and parking. Good wheelchair access. 167 rooms.

Hotel Mirabell $ *Landwehrstrasse 42, 80336 Munich; Tel. (089) 549 17 40; fax (089) 550 37 01.* Good value, family-run hotel just a few minutes walk from the Main Train Station. 68 recently refurbished rooms.

Senefelder Hotel $ *Senefelderstr. 4; Tel. (089) 55 15 40; fax (089) 55 15 4611; e-mail <rezeption@hotel-senefelder.de>.* Reasonably-priced central hotel, with parking. 70 rooms.

THERESIENWIESE

Arabella Sheraton Westpark $$–$$$$ *Garmischer Str. 2; Tel. (089) 51 960; fax (089) 51 96 3000.* Large modern hotel, near exhibition ground and U-Bahn station, with conference rooms, swimming pool, jacuzzi, sauna, restaurant, and cocktail bar. Rooms for disabled and non-smokers, suitable for wheelchair users. 505 beds.

Carmen $$ *Hansastr. 146; Tel. (089) 760 10 99; fax (089) 760 58 43; e-mail <hotel-carmen@t-online.de>.* Quiet hotel southwest of the city center, a short walk from the underground station and 8 minutes from the central station. With parking, restaurant, and conference rooms. 63 rooms.

Garagen-Hotel $ *Lindwurmstr. 20–30; Tel. (089) 544 24 40; fax (089) 544 24 499.* Convenient location for trade fairs and Oktoberfest. Parking available. 40 beds, B&B only.

Hahn Hotel $–$$ *Landsberger Str. 117; Tel. (089) 502 70 37; fax (089) 50 45 86; e-mail <Hotel-Hahn@t-online.de>.* Hotel decorated in the Bavarian-Baroque style, with hospitable and friendly service. Conveniently placed for trade fairs, with sound-proofed windows in 40 rooms, parking, and bar. 70 beds.

Nymphenburg $$ *Nymphenburger Str. 141; Tel. (089) 121 59 70; fax (089) 18 25 40; e-mail <hotel_Nymphenburg@t-online.de>.* Good service in this quiet hotel situated to the north of Theresienwiese, not far from Nymphenburg. Restaurant serving French cuisine, bar, parking. 80 beds.

Seibel $ *Theresienhohe 9; Tel. (089) 540 14 20; fax (089) 540 14 299; e-mail <HotelSeibel@t-online.de>.* Recently-renovated hotel in the Bavarian style. Well situated for the trade fair and Oktoberfest grounds, with parking and sauna. 47 beds, B&B only.

ISAR

Admiral München $$$ *Kohlstr. 9; Tel. (089) 21 63 50; fax (089) 29 36 74; e-mail <info@hotel-admiral.de>.* Situated on the west bank of the Isar near the Deutsches Museum; a short walking distance from the central city sights. Views over the lovely hotel garden, well furnished rooms, some with balcony. Bar and underground parking available. 33 rooms, B&B only.

Hilton Munich City $$$ *Rosenheimer Str. 15; Tel. (089) 48 04 0; fax (089) 48 04 48 04; e-mail <Fon_Munich-City@Hilton.com>.* Near the Gasteig cultural center, conveniently placed for direct transport to the airport. Facilities include restaurants, bar, ballrooms and conference rooms, and garage. Wheelchair access and facilities for disabled guests. 479 rooms.

Forum Hotel $$$$ *Hochstr. 3; Tel. (089) 48 03 0; fax (089) 448 82 77.* Opposite the Gasteig near the Isar, this large hotel has elegant modern décor and all imaginable facilities, including air conditioning, sauna, solarium, swimming pool, hairdresser, car rental, boutiques, conference rooms, and four restaurants. S-bahn station under the hotel. 571 rooms.

Prinzregent $$$$ *Ismaninger Str. 42–44; Tel. (089) 41 60 50; fax (089) 416 054 66; e-mail <Istein@prinzregent.de>.* Exclusive, traditionally decorated, Bavarian style hotel in quiet location near the Isar. Close to underground station and Gasteig. Sauna, bar, parking, conference rooms, non-smoking rooms available. 66 rooms, B&B only.

SCHWABING

Astoria $ *Nikolaistrasse 9; Tel. (089) 383 96 30; fax (089) 383 96 363.* Small hotel just off Leopoldstrasse toward the Englischer Garten. Some parking spaces available; bicycles for rent. 50 beds, B&B only.

Biederstein $ *Keferstr. 18; Tel. (089) 389 99 70; fax (089) 389 99 7389.* Idyllic location on the edge of the Englischer Garten, many rooms with private balcony. Garage available. 45 beds, B&B only.

Holiday Inn Crowne Plaza $$$–$$$$ *Leopoldstrasse 194; Tel. (089) 38 17 90; fax (089) 38 17 98 88.* International hotel with restaurants, bars, swimming pool, sauna and solarium, parking. 6 conference rooms. 644 beds.

Hotel Hauser $ *Schellingstr. 11; Tel. (089) 286 67 50; fax (089) 286 67 599; e-mail <Hotel-Hauser@Munich-info.de>.* Small, attractive, comfortable hotel south of Schwabing, near the University and Englischer Garten, with sauna and solarium, parking. Welcomes children; cots, high chairs etc. available. 34 rooms.

International $$ *Hohenzollernstr. 9; Tel. (089) 39 80 01; fax (089) 39 80 06.* In the heart of Schwabing, just behind Leopoldstrasse; parking. 122 beds, B&B only.

König Ludwig $$$ *Hohenzollernstrasse 3, 80801 Munich; Tel. (089) 33 59 95; fax (089) 39 46 58.* Charming hotel in the lively Schwabing district. Very friendly staff, serving what's claimed to be "Munich's most lovingly-prepared breakfast". 80 rooms.

Mercure Schwabing $ *Leopoldstrasse 120–122; Tel. (089) 39 05 50; fax (089) 34 93 44; e-mail <H1104@accor-hotels.com>.* On Schwabing's main street. Under-ground parking available. 167 rooms, B&B only.

Vitalis $$ *Kathi-Kobus-Str. 20–22; Tel. (089) 12 00 80; fax (089) 12 98 382; e-mail <hotel-vitalis@cybernet-ag.de>.* Friendly hotel below the Olympic Stadium; the large rooms boast good views over Munich. Parking available. Facilities include restaurant, bistro, bar, roof garden, and swimming pool. 145 beds.

Weinfurtner's Garden Hotel $$ *Leopoldstr. 132; Tel. (089) 361 95 70; fax (089) 361 95 76 04.* On Schwabing's main street, with hotel garden, bar and restaurant, conference rooms, and parking. 214 beds, some apartments.

STARNBERGER SEE

Bayerischer Hof $ *Bahnhofsplatz 12, 82319 Starnberg; Tel. (08151) 2750; fax (08151) 12190.* Traditional old hotel, renovated and comfortably furnished. Roof terrace with magnificent views of the lake and Alps, beer garden, and café serving local specialities. Parking available; watersports facilities nearby. Convenient for S-bahn station. 30 rooms

Dorint Hotel Leoni $$ *Assenbucher Str. 44, 82335 Berg-Leoni; Tel. (08151) 5060; fax (08151) 506140.* A modern hotel directly on the edge of the Starnberger See, with balconies in most rooms. Swimming pool, sauna, conference facilities, 2 restaurants, beer garden, and lakeside terrace. 70 rooms.

Kaiserin Elisabeth $–$$ *Tutzinger Str. 2–6, 82340 Feldafing; Tel. (08157) 9309; fax (08157) 930 9133.* Former residence of the Kaiserin Elisabeth; a superb location in parkland on the lakeside, with 18-hole golf course. Bar and popular restaurant with terrace, conference facilities, and tennis. 65 rooms.

Schloß Berg $–$$ *Seestrasse 17, 82335 Berg; Tel. (08151) 963-0; fax (08151) 963 52; e-mail <Hotel.Schloss.Berg@t-online.de>.* Traditional-style hotel on the edge of the Starnberger See, with all modern facilities; sauna, jacuzzi, bicycle rental, large restaurant, and conference rooms. 55 rooms.

Simon $ *Bahnhofsplatz 6, 82131 Gauting; Tel. (089) 850 14 15; fax (089) 850 14 74.* Next to S-bahn station; playground and other facilities for children, sauna and fitness room, free bicycle usage, elevator, parking. 12 rooms.

Tutzinger Hof $ *Tutzinger-Hof-Platz 7, 82319 Starnberg; Tel. (08151) 3081-83; fax (08151) 281-38.* Old established inn, 5 minutes from S-bahn station and lake, with parking, beer garden, and excellent restaurant specializing in Bavarian food and fish dishes. 20 rooms.

LUDWIG'S FOLLIES

Hotel Alte Post $ *Dorfstrasse 19, 82487 Oberammergau; Tel. (08822) 9100; fax (08822) 9101 00.* Charming guesthouse in the picturesque village that's home to the world-famous 10-yearly Passion Play. The building dates back to 1612. It is painted outside in the regional style, and offers warm, rustic Bavarian hospitality. 60 rooms.

Hotel Müller Hohenschwangau $$$ *Alpseestrasse 16 87645 Hohenschwangau; Tel. (0836) 81990; fax (0836) 819913; e-mail <info@hotel-mueller.de>.* Spacious hotel offering elegant accommodations and traditional Bavarian comfort, situated directly below Hohenschwangau Castle. Enjoy a fine meal in the pine-paneled, octagonal restaurant with its view of the castle, or sit in the Wintergarden and savor the magnificent view of Neuschwanstein Castle. 45 rooms.

Hotel Rubezahl $ *Am Ehberg 31, 87645 Schwangau; Tel. (08362) 8327; fax (08362) 81701.* Classic Alpine lodge with fairytale views of Neuschwanstein and Hohenschwangau castles. The interior is wood-paneled and furnished in traditional style. A wide variety of rooms/apartments/suites are offered, and an elaborate buffet breakfast is served. Restaurant, sauna, solarium, whirlpool. 80 rooms.

Keppeler $ *Hauptplatz 15, 86971 Peiting; Tel. (08861) 6201; fax (08861) 66004.* Bavarian-style family inn with restaurant, beer garden and conference room. 25 rooms.

Recommended Restaurants

Munich has a wide range of restaurants, including Hungarian, Italian, French, Greek, and other nationalities. We have tried to cover all areas of the city in our selection, but you will find many of the best restaurants in the Innenstadt or Schwabing. We have included some of the major beer halls and beer gardens in our selection as they are an important focal point of Munich life; they usually serve light meals, snacks, and regional specialities. Please note that in the more expensive restaurants formal dress is expected, including a jacket and tie for men.

The following symbols correspond to the price of a 3-course meal for two people, not including wine.

$$$$	Above DM160
$$$	DM120–160
$$	DM90–120
$	Below DM90

INNENSTADT

Alois Dallmayr $$–$$$ *Dienerstrasse 14–15; Tel. (089) 213 51 00.* Restaurant above the sumptuous delicatessen of the same name, serving not only superb French cuisine but also the classic cake and coffee so beloved by residents of Munich. Open 9:30am-6:30pm Monday–Wednesday, 9:30am-8pm Thursday and Friday and 9:30am-4pm Saturday. No Mastercard.

Andechser am Dom $$ *Weinstrasse 7a; Tel. (089) 29 84 81.* Good value Bavarian specialities and excellent beer served in a friendly atmosphere. No Mastercard.

Augustiner Gaststätten a Neuhauser *Str. 27; Tel. (089) 231 832 57.* Bavarian beer garden serving excellent food, including both Bavarian and international dishes; open every day until midnight. Major credit cards.

Bayerischer Hof Garden Restaurant $$$ *Bayerischer Hof Hotel, Promenadeplatz 2–6; Tel. (089) 2120-0.* Bavarian specialities served in style; in the garden and on the terrace of this exclusive hotel. Major credit cards.

Berni's Nudelbrett $ *Petersplatz 8 (1st floor); Tel. (089) 26 44 69.* Central restaurant, overlooking the Viktualienmarkt, specializing in Italian pasta dishes and steaks. There is also a good selection of wines. Open daily from 11am to 11pm. Major credit cards.

Böttner $$$$ *Pfisterstrasse 9, Tel. (089) 22 12 10.* Old Munich restaurant with an excellent reputation. Specialities include lobster, oysters, caviar, and other seafood. Traditional décor. Closed Sunday. Major credit cards.

Buxs $$ *Frauenstrasse 9; Tel. (089) 22 94 82.* Self-service vegetarian restaurant offering literally dozens of soups and salads. Food is priced by weight. Closed Sunday. No credit cards.

Galleria $$$ *Ledererstrasse 2; Tel. (089) 29 79 95.* Modern Italian food served by cheerful waiters. The walls are decorated with contemporary art. Open evenings only. Closed Sunday. Major credit cards.

Glöckl am Dom $ *Frauenplatz 9; Tel. (089) 29 52 64.* 100-year-old tavern, serving Bavarian specialities and one of the city's best beers. Known particularly for its Nürnberger Bratwurst. No credit cards.

Haxnbauer $$ *Sparkassenstrasse (S. Marienplatz); Tel. (089) 291 621 00.* Old Bavarian tavern specializing in spit-roast meats and regional dishes. Reservations advisable. No Diners Club.

Hofbräuhaus am Platzl $ *Am Platzl 9; Tel. (089) 22 16 76.* The famous Munich beer hall, in traditional Bavarian style, with live brass band music; serves sausages and regional specialities. Mastercard and Visa only.

Hundskugel $$ *Hotterstr. 18; Tel. (089) 26 42 72.* This inn claims to be Munich's oldest; serves good home-cooked Bavarian dishes and grilled meats in a friendly, relaxed atmosphere. No credit cards.

Luigi Tambosi am Hofgarten $$ *Odeonsplatz 18; Tel. (089) 29 83 22.* Eclectic mix of Italian and Austrian dishes in a historic building facing the Feldherrnhalle. The view from the terrace outside is delightful, the atmosphere inside lively. No Diners Club.

Pfälzer Weinprobierstube $ *Residenzstrasse 1; Tel. (089) 22 56 28.* No gourmet cuisine, but good, filling food at reasonable prices. No credit cards.

Prince Myschkin $ *Hackenstr. 2; Tel. (089) 26 55 96; fax (089) 26 44 96.* Spacious and elegant vegetarian restaurant serving imaginative dishes from 11am to midnight every day. Non-smoking tables available. Brunch served on Sunday from 11am to 3pm. Major credit cards.

Ratskeller $$ *Marienplatz 8; Tel. (089) 219 989 24.* Huge labyrinth of an underground restaurant situated, as the name indicates, in the cellar of the Neues Rathaus. You can eat in one of the large rooms with their vaulted ceilings, or choose a more intimate booth. Bavarian cuisine and plenty of beer. Excellent Sunday brunch. Very popular with tourists. Major credit cards.

Spatenhaus an der Opera $$$ *Residenzstrasse 12; Tel. (089) 290 70 60.* Stylish restaurant, furnished in Alpine style, offering Bavarian and international food. No American Express or Diners Club.

Weinstadl $$ *Burgstrasse 5; Tel. (089) 228 074 20.* One of the few Gothic houses left in Munich, this was once the home of the Town Clerk. The orange décor is slightly at odds with the historic building, but the food is good (traditional fare with a modern twist) and the atmosphere lively. In the summer, eating in the garden by the fountain is a pleasure. No Visa.

Zum Alten Markt $$ *Dreifaltigkeitsplatz 3; Tel. (089) 29 99 95.* Popular restaurant decorated in hunting-lodge style, adjacent to the Viktualienmarkt. The grilled meats and salads are particularly good. Reservations recommended. Closed Sunday. No credit cards.

AROUND KARLSPLATZ

Augustinerkeller $ *Arnulfstr. 52; Tel. (089) 59 43 93.* Attractively-shaded Bavarian-style beer garden serving Wurst and traditional regional snacks with good beer. No credit cards.

Königshof $$$$ *Karlsplatz 25; Tel. (089) 55 13 60.* Elegant restaurant serving mainly quality French cuisine, with pleasant views over Karlsplatz. Reservations required. Major credit cards.

Opus One $ *Seidlstr. 18; Tel. (089) 55 76 81.* Just northwest of the station, this restaurant serves sophisticated Californian food and wines and a range of American-style snacks and sandwiches. Open until 11pm. Closed Saturday lunch and Sunday. Major credit cards.

THERESIENWIESE

Canton $$$ *Theresienstr. 49; Tel. (089) 52 21 85.* Popular Chinese restaurant; good food and service. Open 11:30am–3pm and 5:30–11:30pm. Major credit cards.

Glockenbach $$$ *Kapuzinerstr. 29; Tel. (089) 53 40 43.* Popular restaurant specializing in Bavarian and French-style cuisine made with fresh fish and game. Closed Sunday and Monday. Reservations required. No Diners Club.

Gundel $$$ *Hungar-Hotel, Paul-Heyse Str. 24; Tel. (089) 51 49 00.* One of the famous chain of Hungarian restaurants; quality Hungarian dishes in a friendly atmosphere. Major credit cards.

Italfisch $$$ *Zenettistrasse 25; Tel. (089) 77 68 49.* Outstanding seafood and superb service prove an unbeatable combination that's well worth the high prices. Open 11:30am-3pm and 6pm-1am Monday-Friday, and 6pm to 1am Saturday. Closed Sunday. No Diners Club.

Kleinschmidtz $–$$ *Fraunhoferstrasse 13; Tel. (089) 260 85 18.* Good-value restaurant and wine shop serving organic food.

The décor consists of constantly changing art exhibits. Closed Sunday lunchtime. No credit cards.

La Fiorentina $$ *Goethestr. 41; Tel. (089) 53 41 85.* Freshly made, good quality Italian food and ambiance. Closed Thursday. Major credit cards.

Paulaner Bräuhaus $ *Kapuzinerplatz 5; Tel. (089) 544 61 10.* Traditional working brewery and beer garden serving home-brewed beer (what else?) and excellent local cuisine. Very popular with the local workers, who frequent it at lunchtime. Major credit cards.

Pschorrkeller $ *Theresienhöhe 7; Tel. (089) 50 10 88.* Typical Bavarian beer garden. Major credit cards.

ISAR

Brasserie $$ *Arabellastr. 5, Bogenhausen; Tel. (089) 923 244 33.* Bistro meals, buffet, and popular Sunday brunch in the Arabella Hotel, Bogenhausen. Major credit cards.

El Espagnol $ *Pariserstr. 46; Tel. (089) 48 84 96.* Beyond the Gasteig center, off Rosenheimer Strasse. A well-known, lively Spanish restaurant serving all the popular dishes. Open daily 5pm–1am. Major credit cards.

Käferschenke $$$ *Schwannstr. 73, Bogenhausen; Tel. (089) 416 80.* Specializes in fresh fish dishes. Outdoor dining, rustic and period furnishings; closed Sunday. Reservations recommended. Major credit cards.

Kam Yi $ *Rosenheimerstr. 32; Tel. (089) 448 136 601.* Popular Chinese restaurant across the road from the Gasteig Center. Open until midnight. Major credit cards.

Rue des Halles $$ *Stein str. 18; Tel. (089) 48 56 75.* A bistro-type restaurant serving quality French food. No American Express.

Weisses Bräuhaus $ *Tal. 7; Tel. (089) 29 98 75.* Bavarian-style beer hall specializing in Weißbier; also the best place to go for Weisswurst. Open 8:30am to midnight. No credit cards.

SCHWABING

Bamburger Haus $$$ *Brunnerstrasse 2 (at Luitpold Park); Tel. (089) 308 89 66.* Restaurant and brewery hall in an 18th century palace with beautiful terrace in the park. Traditional Bavarian food. Major credit cards.

Chinesischer Turm $ *Englischer Garten 3; Tel. (089) 383 87 30.* One of Munich's first and largest beer gardens—with traditional live oompah music—serving the typical Bavarian snacks. Major credit cards.

Halali $$ *Schönfeldstr. 22; Tel. (089) 28 59 09.* Traditional Munich restaurant serving Bavarian dishes and also imaginative new German cuisine using local ingredients. Good service. Reservations recommended. Closed Saturday lunchtime, Sundays, and bank holidays. Major credit cards.

Italy $ *Leopoldstr. 108; Tel. (089) 34 64 03.* Good quality but basic Italian food, mainly pasta and pizzas. Major credit cards.

Max-Emanuel-Brauerei $ *Adalbert Str. 33; Tel. (089) 271 51 58.* Small beer hall serving typical Bavarian fare. Live music and lively atmosphere. No Mastercard or American Express.

Osterwaldgarten $$ *Keferstrasse 12; Tel. (089) 384 050 40.* Renovated restaurant and beer garden at the Englischer Garten. Good food and beer, though not bargain prices. No credit cards.

Tantris $$$ *Johann-Fichte-Str. 7; Tel. (089) 361 95 90; fax (089) 361 84 69.* Superb nouvelle cuisine served in a modern restaurant with stark and startling modern décor. Outdoor dining. Closed Sunday and Monday. Reservations essential. Major credit cards.

Werneckhof $$ *Wernckstr. 11; Tel. (089) 39 99 36.* An elegant French restaurant with Bavarian décor; serves a range of good, freshly-cooked dishes. No credit cards.

STARNBERGER SEE

Andechser Hof $$ *Haupster. 25, Tutzing; Tel. (08158) 1822.* Bavarian-style restaurant and large beer garden serving quality food, mainly local specialties.

Dorint Hotel Leoni $ *Assenbucher Str. 44, Berg-Leoni; Tel. (08151) 5060.* A modern hotel and restaurant with an attractive lakeside terrace. Major credit cards.

Kaiserin Elisabeth $ *Tutzinger Str. 2–6, Feldafing; Tel. (08157) 9309.* Popular restaurant with terrace overlooking the park and lake. Major credit cards.

Schloß Berg $ *Seestrasse 17, 82335 Berg; Tel. (08151) 9630.* Large restaurant, lakeside terrace. Major credit cards.

Tutzinger Hof $$$ *Tutzinger-Hof-Platz 7, Starnberg; Tel. (08151) 3081.* This 16th-century Bavarian-style inn also has an excellent restaurant that specializes in hearty Bavarian food and fish dishes. The beer garden is pleasant. Major credit cards.

LUDWIG'S FOLLIES

Buchberger $$ *Füssener Str. 2, Peiting; Tel. (08861) 6266.* Fresh Weißwürste available on Fridays, also international cuisine, salad buffet. Major credit cards.

Müller $$ *Alpseestrasse 16, Hohenschwangau; Tel. (0836) 81990.* Fine regional food served in the welcoming, pine-paneled octagonal restaurant of this charming hotel. Enjoy excellent views of Hohenschwangau Castle. No American Express.

Zum Dragoner $$ *Ammergauer Str. 11, Peiting; Tel. (08861) 25070.* Well-known restaurant specializing in fish and game; good selection of wine. Major credit cards.

Zum Pinzger $$ *Am Hauptplatz, 9, Peiting; Tel. (08861) 6240.* Popular restaurant specializing in game, grilled meat, fish, and home-made sausages. Has a pleasant, shaded beer garden. No credit cards.

INDEX